Gradus ad Phlegethon

D.A.R.G.

Published by Yperion Press, 2024.

GRADUS AD PHLEGETHON

First edition. March 21, 2024.

Copyright © 2024 D.A.R.G..

ISBN: 979-8224251933

Written by D.A.R.G..

ACKNOWLEDGEMENTS

The writing of this volume would not have been possible without the collaboration and inspiration of Brett Stevens and Rex Ebvleb. It is by their generosity in thought and communication, as well as in their written contributions here in the form of interviews, that this volume acquires the value and weight necessary to merit publishing. I am also doubly indebted to G.K.M.M. for her support and practical guidance throughout the writing process. Without her, none of this would have survived the periodic floods of desperation and destruction.

CONTENTS

INTRODUCTION

The present volume attempts to present what the author has until now formulated with regards to a vision of metal music as a proper conduct for the sinister, that is, as an authentic dark musick. It is not so much an attempt to explain what is, as to highlight the best amongst it in regards to a perceived sinister esoteric essence on the one hand, but also musical efficacy empirically tested. The nature of such an effort is limited to the individual presenting these ideas and opinions.

The sequence of propositions, explanations and conceptualizations are presented primarily through a loose methodological and conceptual abstraction with the aim to enhance the experiential practice, bringing it under control. They are not meant to be definitive, but rather to be worked upon as avenues for growth brought into conscious awareness. Such a step in the making of decidedly dark musick in the metal vein would signify a shift in evolution that abandons the mystical, that which seeks for inexplicable and unquestionable mystique, and that which is grounded in understanding, yet not devoid, but effectively leading to an evocation or invocation of the sinisterly-numinous.

The first section, A Vision of Darkness, is a condensed draft of an originally much longer document elaborated throughout the years 2016 and 2017. It is a description of the origins of black metal from a musical perspective, while in the meantime gleaning into it an interpretation of the aural tradition that has grown in and through underground metal in general, and within black metal more specifically. Moreover, this has been filtered to leave out the melodramatic and self-deluding —the Crowlean delusions that have hitherto been the staple of those adhering to the name of the musical genre.

The second section, A Sorcerous Craft, is half the length of the first, and is in essence a proposition for the handling of riffphrases in metal as fluxions as explained by Anton Long in the Sinister Tradition. The conclusion is to take the idea of possession and ritual in metal not merely allegorically, but to acquire an abstract understanding from experience into further, conscious application.

We are honoured and proud to feature an interview with Ebvleb of Abyssum, alongside an introductory short essay under the name of Ars Symphonica. The number and nature of diverse collocations that have lead such a collaboration to be possible are so fortuitous, so synchronistic, as to cause any one to ascribe it all to an incredible chance. Others may yet see something else, unnameable perhaps, at work through and in the individuals involved.

Much of what is presented throughout, especially in A Vision of Darkness, owes its birth, inspiration, sense of direction and nature to the writings of Brett Stevens. And so, it seems perfectly adequate, if not mandatory, to this author to include an interview with him that adds a great deal of weight to the contents of this publication. The interview, titled Esoteric Nihilism, is introduced with a brief article that attempts to discuss various comparisons between other works and Brett Stevens' book Nihilism.

A VISION OF DARKNESS

PRAELUDIUM

The present work's end is to bring about a new and higher conception of black metal art as a way to dark spirituality. It is not presumed that such a feat may be brought about by this single enterprise alone. However, the sewing of seeds in the right soil may, in time, sprout a sapling which will become a robust oak of deep roots and overarching greenery. Such an organism would be the incarnation of a futurist culture determined by a post-nihilistic super-spirituality —one that it has gone through phases of annihilation and rebirth.

In a sterile society, young artists with an insatiable appetite for life and a yearning for knowledge of what underlies our mundane existences readily, hasten art towards its inevitable consequences. Metal approached this doom in a form of dark beauty and inverted symbols within the span of fifteen years. Raw, superficial modifications had produced a rapid evolution of aesthetics whose curve was akin to a gradual depuration. The confusion which thereafter ensued was a testament to Death's arrival, as all started to crumble. The budding metal movement was about to endure its first dark age, one which would span the same amount of time that had taken Black Metal to arise as the form which mirrored its innermost essence.

If we expect a dynamic and natural movement, that is, one that is in constant becoming, then past encumbrances embedded in tradition itself must be shed. We must move beyond both the powerful yet uncontrolled rage of intuitive channeling that gave rise to a golden era of classic works, and the disgraceful years of barren utilitarianism and technicality that followed. The admixture of internal and external, theoretical and practical, rational and emotional, and conscious and unconscious, reveals a holistic path. If we are to make use of the whole of our faculties to achieve our ends, we may not as artists disregard the intellect, nor as scientists lay aside intuition.

For black metal art in its current state, it implies the apparition of a different sphere, a more conceptualized one that allows for versatility below and focus above. Black metal artists in the past have attained such a vision through an individual illumination, but this could be part of the teachings within atradition, a living tradition and not a set of petrified rules which demand to be followed; we must point rather towards a collected body of wisdom acquired through experience and insight. Here lies a being born of torment, assembled from the shards of a broken spiritual husk and paid for by the shedding of a soul's blood; but with Death comes Temperance, and a chance for Renewal.

FOUNDATIONS

Archetypal Origins in Black Sabbath

BLACK SABBATH PUBLISHED their first album in the midst of a rising tide of popular interest in the occult. This countercultural gesture was in truth a reaction to the emptiness and corruption perceived as inherent to civilization in our times. The generation who came of age two decades after the second of the World Wars was defined by the apparent truth created by that catastrophic event. To understand the cultural implications of such events, we must be able to see how the results of the conflict, and not only the conflict in itself, was a terrible thing for humanity.

As the twentieth century progressed from the catastrophe of World War II towards the end of the Cold War, young people in contact with reality sensed a discrepancy between what they were told by society and what was apparent to them. There arose a deep suspicion of a hidden reality that was being purposefully covered up by those around them; a reality which, if uncovered, could lead to liberation from the slowly consuming and spiritually void husk of the modern world.

Even though only a relatively small number of individuals remotely understood the symbols and riddles of the occult, or at least cared enough to take an interest in them, a dark traditional influence over Western European culture could be traced back to pre-historic times; its hold over the collective unconscious was and continues to be such that its symbols never ceased to be the inner language of the West. What was now known as the occult was a perversion of what had been a living tradition that had taken different shapes and forms but whose concepts preserved primordial germs of a cosmogonic view. Druids, witches and such had preserved the esoteric line of inheritance, ensuring the survival of teachings while putting into action these principles in temporary exoteric forms.

The occult renaissance that spilt from the nineteenth century onto the twentieth was no mere fashion tide, but the revival of something which had always lingered under, not yet dead because an intrinsic part of what is European; what had really changed was that, while during the years of almost absolute Christian control the status quo considered it a danger to its own interests, the new presumptuously materialist reigning paradigm simply brushed it off as irrelevant.

Modernity as a result of the so-called Enlightenment has always been a paradox: enabled by the material benefits of industrialism, it was launched on a quest to rediscover and redefine itself spiritually beyond the petrified state in which religion found itself at the time. The obsession with the occult which became a mainstream phenomenon in the midst of the Cold War could be said to be an echo of that Romantic era. The original romantic spirit from more than a century before was a push against despotism and mechanistic cruelty; it had arisen as a horror stricken sensitive soul that saw the gradual tearing apart of a beautiful creation. The new sentiment was caused by a much graver ordeal which verged on the apocalyptic. The revival brought a form of the older Romantic ideals back, but on a more superficial level, and was instead defined by an element surely caused by a much more sterile and explicitly threatening world: an extreme apathy, a sense of desperation beyond all hope for recovery and a premonition of calamity which spelt finality for our kind.

Out of this bleak landscape first arose metal, and its first manifestations came through Black Sabbath. In these we hear the innate metaphysician and mystic whose innate intelligence and developed skill lead him to inspect and tear down the social subterfuge that surrounds him part by part by whatever means are available to him. In Black Sabbath it is not the voice of trained philosophers, adepts or theologians that we hear, but that of the man with un-common sense facing a dreadful reality through the symbols that tradition has utilized to preserve information.

In Black Sabbath's lyrics we find a statement of crude reality, but not a condemnation of it per se. It is the human being himself who is constantly accused of weakness when placed in a world of fear and decadence that is suddenly revealed. Metal did not appeal to euphemisms nor believed the end of the world could be wished away; drugs were not embraced as a source of true happiness nor were they vituperated. Few people have understood the true meaning underlying the message of metal as a whole, which essentially has been that the problem of humanity is its own denial of reality and not the objects and ideas with which it becomes obsessed.

We must understand that popular expressions of one sort or another are only permitted when they are not deemed dangerous to the status quo. Metal contains the essence of a realist's thoughts which are poison to a delusional civilization, but it has survived for the same reason that ancient myths survive: it lies covered by layers of indirection. Myth is a symbolic vehicle that amplifies and penetrates those minds that are fertile ground for the seeds of a message to grow.

We may, without a shadow of doubt, affirm that Black Sabbath's music as a first manifestation of metal was the only truly dark music transiting along popular channels. Preceding them were the so-called occult rock bands, which many would name as proof of the contrary. Such allegations are justified in their claim that there were artists with considerably more profound, darker and clearer understanding and projecting of occult concepts at a time before the birth of heavy metal. The error lies in mistaking intent for the music itself, and in confusing the expression of the lyrics with the actual content of the music.

It must be made clear that the words of a song themselves are extraneous to the music, though they are intimately related to the same source of inspiration, whatever that may truly be, and serve only as directors of attention. It is the melodic line on the shoulders of which they are carried which in truth is a part of the music itself. There is no absolute assurance in the transmission of information and translation of energy, so that the artist can claim certitude in the knowledge of the origin of what he channels.

There may be more evil in music that transpires tension, heaviness and fear through the actual harmony in movement and textures, even though the accompanying words reveal only a surface or a set of symbols without their understanding. On the other hand, Satanic musings and deep insights of an occultist intellectual that are carried by a music of a much more light-hearted character that is not musically differentiable from mundane popular production can make no claims to the effectiveness or profoundness of the music itself, but only of the words and the intent of their writer.

Anything coming into existence is invariably the result of forces and influences present and acting before them. So it is that in Black Sabbath's music we hear the mannerisms of blues and rock, as well as the energetic blasts of hard rock which would eventually become a defining feature of heavy metal. There was a third great musical influence which pervaded this new genre to its very marrow yet at the same time in a subtle ways which have not been properly acknowledged with a correct understanding of the matter.

Said influence was the motif-driven horror movie music which leaned on the longer phrases of classical music of the romantic period. Popular movie music was, of course, simpler than the old ivory tower art, and was made with the purpose of transmitting clear impressions to an audience rather being the subject matter of intellectual debate. Black Sabbath's integration of riff and melody into a phrase as train of thought within the context of heavy rock instrumentation was to become the bedrock of metal music.

Critical to the superior quality of minimalist acts of dark beauty were the structures Black Sabbath adopted in their first two releases primarily, which were not the standard verse and chorus compositions. Black Sabbath's songs are not constructed from a haphazard appending of riffs, they achieve a comparatively long duration in letting each section speak at the appropriate speed, tasting every note and phrase as it is necessary while introducing a new idea before natural momentum has been spent. Within each section they may display either one repetition of an alternating pair, or a recursion of the larger structure; the heavy and more lasting effect of such concrete decisions should not be underestimated.

There are two characteristics Black Sabbath boasts of which lend to its particular transmission of a sense of heaviness. In Iommi's tendency to use of both extremes of the guitar neck we find the first of these. He would often play high and low notes in rapid juxtaposition within a same section or even within a same riff-phrase; the effect thus achieved is one of tension and destabilizing motion from jump in frequency and the associated momentum that will be either be allowed to continue or must be opposed virulently and with great impact to change its course. The use of middle frequencies is more measured and notes played in this area tend to provide a stronger sense of stability as a result of consistently more moderate usage.

A second and more subtle cause is found in the way spacing across time is managed, that is, not tempo only but note-length. Iommi will allow for whole notes, and sometimes white notes, with a few quavers to round off the very end of the consequent in phrases using a period form; it must be added here that metal seems to be incredibly fond of the period form, and it is yet another element in the legacy that classical music passed on to the genre through Black Sabbath. The treatment of the organization of notes within phrases provides plenty of room for expansion and variation within a tight musical concept, and it is also, perhaps, more of a rediscovery of basic musical possibilities arising from immutable principles than a direct borrowing.

Even though drums certainly emphasize heaviness in the same way that those of heavy rock do, it is usually achieved through the use of sheer force and simplicity. Ward hybridizes these by admixture with a jazz-like swing and technicality, proficiently choosing the moment to use one or the other approach, thereby giving us a premonition of a synthesis beyond both that would invade the realms of death metal. In so doing, Ward, the drummer, defines a new kind of backdrop in percussion for Iommi's clever phrases.

Foundations in Bathory

IN QUORTHON'S MUSIC we see a more convincing proposal for diabolical music that goes beyond the widespread predilection of metal artists for the mythic and the obscure. The shadow that looms over an early Black Sabbath steps forward as a consummated invocation in the presence of Bathory. The older group crossed lines while dancing back and forth in a nebulous space open to a certain manner of interpretation, but Bathory displayed an unmistakable, devil-worship music with the spiritual overtones of a European tradition bespeaking of influences called upon through the elements of nature under the moon and the intrinsic physical influences these have over human beings.

The dark presence, the Horned God, is no longer acknowledged and recognized only as a powerful influence, but he is called and presenced. In the words of Varg Vikernes: music is sorcery. Bathory's second work could be, in light of this last reflection, considered a satanic hymn book. Furthermore, the particular way in which Quorthon writes about these concepts echoes the sentiment of the European Witch-Cult as depicted by Margaret Alice Murray in her The God of the Witches, tying it to land and thence a deep spirituality. Here, Quorthon serves as bard and prophet of The Devil as sentient cosmic force, recounting experience in life as testimony and looking into the future through signs of unrest.

To understand this voluntary embrace of evil as lying beyond simple egotistical caprice, one must abandon any anthropomorphic conceptions of beings of a higher order that are commonly espoused by the profane; this much should be made clear before we can proceed, although this is not the place for theological discussions on the subject of considerable length.

There is in the lyrical content of The Return of Darkness and Evil a welcoming of an apocalyptic onslaught and upheaval. For what reason this is so conceived in the mind of the acolyte, we are not told. The uplifting of destructive force, the outbreak of natural forces or human passions may be taken as one more way of worshipping a pure form of Darkness. On second thought, however, we discover that the converse may also be true; this is an illusion behind which lies the evident idea hidden in plain sight: that they are both one and the same. It is not a blind force of nature nor is it a personality encased in ego; it is sentient cosmic force, a higher order of being, existing beyond common conceptions. Bathory makes this quite patent in recounting this presencing through the senses of an influence possessed of Will which appears all around but is not what it appears to be.

Worship of sacred darkness preserves the transcendent bent of Europe's old religion, while emphasizing elitism probably to an even greater degree than tradition originally did. To be sure, elitism does not necessarily imply a higher excellence, but denser filter. The idea behind this theory is that to address a problem, the solution cannot come in a form that is incompatible to it but must rather respond to it and speak back at the appropriate level.

Human life is not seen as sacred, but only as a stage of opportunity and probation. For if the soul is immortal or, more properly in line with pre-classical European tradition, if immortality can be achieved through the transmutation of the basic soul unit, then whence the sanctity of this carnal state?

Evil becomes a synonym for unleashed Force, or that which carries forth creative energies of dissolution; and so, unbound, breaks across limits.

Out of all the elements which come to define black metal ideologically, free will and a staunch refusal to acknowledge any form of authority are universally recognized as its prime movers. It is often incorrectly assumed that for music to transmit chaos, then it must itself become chaos, while the point should be to transmit the experience of chaos to the mind of the listener; correction lies in the clear perception of the inner traits of art.

What black metal did for metal on the musical level was quite the opposite of what the more recent penchant for wild experimentation shows. Instead of outer extravagance, we find simplicity, and instead of anarchist vituperation, elitist reservation. In The Return of Darkness and Evil, the creator behind the music reins in the instruments and redirects them as a pointed lance towards a clear path. It may be a path of debauchery and evil, perhaps, but one that fulfils its promise. Thus, there is an effort to focus the whole in the name of an idea to a degree that had not been attempted in the history of metal. To erect an edifice of any kind, a channelling of energies must occur in a concrete way, even if the subject matter of the art be free and chaotic.

Guitars function as short carriers of motifs which through expression (id est, tremolo picking, strumming direction and intensity) emphasize energy, vivacity or repose, as befits the occasion. In their traditional black metal usage, the central guitar is lightning, it is fire and expansion; like fire, or more properly, the essence of it, it must comprehend a flow and its rupturing of space must conform to natural laws that dictate the possibilities of this path. And because minimalist, music relies on the guitar for its proper sense of melodic cadence; freedom lies in how this is accomplished, but accomplished it must be. The guitar solo and the guitar line cease to be important personalities distinct from the rest, and becomes an extension of the character behind the music, a flicker amongst enormous energies in movement.

Drums are reduced to what some like to refer to as a metronome, but which are in truth the principal agents in charge of modulating texture. In this extremely abrasive, minimalist music, the drummer must strive to strike a balance between being the source of a constant flow of energy that sustains the strength of the whole and a sensitive receptor of both explicit and implicit gestures of the music, to then go beyond both and become what comes to life around the guitar line. Black metal drums are a monolithic organic mesh that expands and contracts by the needs of the developing spirit of the work; it becomes in the superior work of black metal the principal element that defines texture through percussive density, timber and quality in a way that is unique to the genre.

Vocals follow the example set by Black Sabbath by adhering rhythmically to the guitar lines, riding them, flattening against them, while at the same time amplifying and rounding certain contours. While vocal performance may come to be seen as unnecessary or even too rudimentary, the early work of Bathory gives us a hint of how it acts as a modifier of context; it is a kind of auditory seasoning that punctuates the narrative of the music and which can even be used to immensely enhance the expressive power of the whole as it funnels or diverts attention towards areas of sound frequency or moments in the music.

The outer is only useful insofar as it leads deeper inside. And the inner insofar as it reveals the outside universe. It is about discovering the mystery in every being, in the self, not for a mundane purpose, but to go beyond and above all that is merely human. Black metal alludes to this precisely in that it is only in relation to that transcendence that each of the instruments attains meaning of consequence that allows it to supersede banality.

Incessant blast beats throughout minutes uninterrupted by anything but cymbals for emphasis or adornment would normally appear as nonsensical in any other context. Correctly understood in this holistic art, however, they become a vessel for multiform purposes and reasoning. Bathory did not make use of blast beats, but the application of the same concept with older, more conservative percussion techniques was already laid out in The Return of Darkness and Evil. Textures here may become so uniform as to give an impression of a lack of content, and it is only in the recognizing of significances in the individual instruments that the door is opened to rich variations and eloquent expositions of dark and pensive trains of thought.

Hereby are the instruments sublimated, directed with purpose to a higher sphere, leaving their expression an intangible essence which forces us to step back and see shapes form and be destroyed amidst their interaction. The guitar gains propulsion as percussion provides, while the latter sees its own movement bearing unimaginable fruit on the peaks of the guitars and synths supported upon it. This act of purification and ennoblement, if we may use such a term here, is not an abstract idea to be applied to any context or readily attached to any meaning. Its great power comes from being fundamentally fused with a so-called evil intent and mongering, the discussion of which yields abstruseramifications that will appear contradictory to profane understanding. It is in transcending mere functionality and becoming united with meaning that the parts are melted and the whole enhanced in their name.

ELITISM

WHATEVER WE MAY SAY black metal is, it certainly is individualistic and existentialist. Individualism is here an outlook that considers development to be a path on which he is alone, and alone he is responsible for it; in such a definition, there is no intention of alluding to that egotistic attitude of selfindulgence an blindness beyond petty selfish concerns.

Each and every attempt to understand the attitudes and approach, both in music-making as craft and as a transcendent work of art, of black metal takes us back to the highly discriminatory attitude it presents in almost every respect. There is in it an utter disrespect for almost any institution or ideology that cannot be seen as reasserting itself explicitly against weakness; which weakness is vehemently scorned and is of a spiritual and mental kind.

Self-reliance and individual worth as a result of proven mettle through strife are so essential that every aspect of black metal appears designed as a set of tests or veils that cover the grain of its underlying proposition or truth. Like traditional esoteric layering, the levels of indirection themselves contain valuable information and are beautifully wrought in their own way. Unlike other traditions, however, black metal is more of an incidental surfacing of symbols and methods that organically emerged from a closed collective mentality.

Respect and prominence is given to those who rise above the merely human. A point should be made of clearly perceiving the nuance that sets this spiritual elitism from the simple echoing of might as right. On the other hand, a decisive violence embraced transcendentally is part of which black metal embodies beyond morality.

Themes

WITH RESPECT TO EVERY artistic movement there can be defined a set of themes, the expression of which ultimately becomes music. Black metal is an explicit counter culture which, while clearly at odds with modernism, is forward-looking and individualist. The focus of this particular ethos revolves around the experience of the individual and the presencing of forces and patterns behind manifestation. The garment worn by black metal, possibly unbeknownst to those original musicians who planted its seeds, related to transcendental ideas that would inspire the building of towers reaching towards metaphysical heights.

At the root of everything lay the spirit of a former romantic idealist gone rogue, turned into a misanthropist by the realization that most humans are not only delusional, but that they are so willingly. There can be glimpsed in the development of black metal artists, moreover, the realization of a path as a first stage in an esoteric journey that would rise through the seven spheres, to the solar, and thence further.

This understanding of reality as a particular choice of occult tendencies favoured the heretical and had as a prerequisite an alienation from modern civilization and society, thereby developing and extreme form of mental independence. It was assumed that the truthful individual was defined by his action in reality. Furthermore, and in accordance with traditionally occult principles, it was and is deemed proper to keep one's plans and activities to oneself. It should not be assumed that it is being implied that this is the way everyone who is said to be a black metal musician has behaved this way, but that a reading into the attitudes, message and music as a whole speaks of this as its essence.

Music was composed not with the audience in mind, but with the intention of artists behind it producing some kind of medium, as a connection to the cosmos, that others may catch a glimpse of that experience through the concrete arrangement of notes. It was assumed that the person who was to receive them should have the capacity to perceive them properly, even if not immediately, with intuitive discernment as well as a will and patience to delve into abysmal obscurity.

Literacy

LITERACY AS IT IS USED here, refers to having learned from written sources which stretch back in time and across the globe the necessary concepts and symbols that guide towards a more detailed and enriched path that is knowledgeable and not only aurally experienced. That is, a certain level of internalised education, whatever its source, is perhaps not absolutely necessary but, in this day and age, almost certainly a given amongst individuals who discover such things through their own explorations since even fewer still could even hope to have a link with an ancient living tradition of this sort.

We must here turn our attention to a widespread mischaracterisation of the Left Hand Path, which has some to adopt a deeply anti-intellectual attitude. The pretext behind such an attitude appears to lie in the conviction that the rational mind will mislead in an excess of rationalizations. It should be clear from this that the proper application of literacy could have rescued those with the innate capacity to, sooner or later, look beyond deceptions and mirages of the kind.

The mythological bent of black metal, and the metaphysical implications which alone aid its attaining of holistic value, also imply the necessity of literacy. Discovery must still happen individually, but finding the door, even when the existence of such a door is at least suspected, takes the re-building of what esoteric traditions have already refined through generations of trial and error.

Obscurantism

THE OBSCURANTISM OF black metal pertains a deliberate withholding of information from the general audience. The intention is to avoid wasting energy and resources on an unworthy majority; in so doing, certain esoteric principles are upheld, whether on purpose or otherwise. The use of such an esoteric method attempts to make understanding blossom within the receiver, receptor or student, rather than providing direct information in any explicit manner.

Delivering content through an obscurantist method opens up the person trying to glimpse through it to thoughts and images that are produced within him entirely by seeds are procured elsewhere. The seed of that knowledge has always been within, existing and latent within the individual, the exterior only functions as stimulus. Instead of imposing another way of seeing the world, it turns the listener into a traveller walking into the universe within their selves.

The twist here is that it is acknowledged that reason alone is not as powerful as the whole of the mind. We need both intuition and reason; we need the feminine as much as we need the masculine within us. Hence we get the purposeful stimulation and obfuscation of elements in works of art. Instead, true art needs both in order to be accessed in its entirety.

Obscurantism, then, also acknowledges the multiplicity of paths that lead to perceptions of truth which amount to reality perceived from different angles. True works of black metal are made with such concentrated thought and intention through natural presencing, that when channelled correctly, when translated into music with an adept dominion of the craft, results in a nucleus of energy and codified communication that takes time, thought, feeling and experience outside it to be brought into focus.

In purposeful obfuscation and hiding away there is not only the veiling from the profane and the unprepared, but also a code which contains the key. It takes one who would tread its overgrown paths, one who would ponder upon it and lie on its meadows, times without end.

Experience as Trial

THOSE WHO CAN ONLY see brute aggression and primal impulses, impulses which paralyse him with fear, or make him turn away in disgust, form part of the first filtered layer of mundane minds. If one is able to accept the nature of the beast and his actions in a detached way then here is a sign of potential. But it is profound empathy with the trials and proceeding of the wild being that marks those who belong to the sinister path. It is in recognising in a part of ourselves a pure will to survive and overcome, that we connect to an inner being which has lain dormant within us.

To become civilised is to come under external control, to be domesticated. The spirit of black metal spirit sees in giving in a great weakness that is at the very base of all modern complacency and mediocrity. While the modern individual is not able to truly see himself as separate and against the artificial environment that surrounds him, he will not be able to reach the beginning of a lycanthropic transmutation.

Black metal spirit as arising and adhering to a maturing adversarial philosophy alienated from the values of modern civilisation sees in direct experience with one's own darker, hidden and wild nature are the working matter of Alchemy. Dark experiences may be of many kinds, though they must involve a degree of reflection after a raw apprehension of shocking life experience or some other path which has led to an altered state of consciousness.

Given these elements of the black path, there is a connection between them and the lunar and muliebrial qualities found in old European cults or those explained and incorporated by Hinduism as the sensitive and cunning sacred feminine. Personal experience and individual judgement are considered to be the highest authority. It is of utmost importance to have one's own perception acquired through exercised intuition and reflection. Hence the wilful obscurantism; hence the silence; hence the belief that only individual discovery and development driven by a strong will constitutes true worth.

A MUSIC OF DARK SPIRITUALITY

Aggression and Veiling

ONE OF THE FOREMOST characteristics of black metal is that besides being abrasive in an intentional manner in order to deter certain kind of people from peering in, and luring a different kind of soul towards its depths, it covers itself with a mantle of distortion. It is clear that there is in this the function of aggression, but it also constitutes a first ring of protection around the mystery. For black metal does not simply sing about the mystery, but is, at its deepest and most honest, in itself a mystery tradition of lonely wanderers.

Even when the initial shock is absorbed and its raw impact accepted, distortion serves the function of both obfuscating and enriching content. What we would normally consider the sound artifacts of distortion come to form an important part of the identity of this music itself. It is not its defining quality as some would have it, however, as that must be found in a collective understanding of its musical construction methods as well as in a nuanced apprehension of the living culture that sustains it.

By this obfuscation, then, a greater and more beautiful art is born. It is not beautiful because it is veiled, but because the veiling material is itself created through great artistry and communicates its own layer of meaning. The labyrinth is also a test and a defence against the profane, however, it amplifies and reinforces meaning for those worthy of it.

As one delves deeper and further into black metal, the symbols and archetypes give way to pure sensations and intimation to those who connect to it so that they ride and move through the movement of the music without imposition. This knowing comes acausally rather than causally since it is not time or explanations which make this stepping past the veils possible, but an affinity and letting go when the listener's own mind has seen some transmutation. The degree to which this change occurs dictates the kind of intimation which may be had.

The spirit of black metal stands behind all of these apparently contrasting manifestations, and these are each but windows, through which each individual, by their own dispositions, and interpreted according to adeptness, brings about intimations of a primordial knowing, the static that cuts through and vivifies and destroys. The Left Hand Path tread by black metal could be compared to that unspoken tradition that presenced raw Nature directly and without recourse to abstractions.

Stepping further into the layers of conceptual veiling also allows us to attempt an un-covering of the spiritual motions of the music. Aggression and misanthropy soon give way to idealism in a music redolent of painful empathy. Empathy of this dark form is, furthermore, holistic and heroic, and therefore supra-personal. Nihilism, which also shows itself in what first appears to be an unexplained destructive impetus, is rather a kind of doorway to be crossed as part of a process of self-immolation.

The listener who is able to burn his sensations through the fire of this rough exterior undergoes a similar process. Innate power for intimation and empathy is required, but also a conscious hunger for experience besides, and learning in an alternating rhythm that oscillates between a patient letting go and a wilful pushing forth.

Imperfection as Being and Seeming

ECHOING MANIFEST REALITY, black metal brings forth patterns and motifs in repeated riffs, but it does not try to make every single instance of a riff and note identical to those that came before it even when engaged within repetition of a same shape. This irregularity gives rise to a numinous identity that affords each moment a character of its own in the midst of its singular location.

When we refer to black metal as raw, the implication is that it is unprocessed, and thus closer to its original state and nature. It is not precisely alive on its own, for the sounds of life do not conform to human-made music. It is rather music which attempts to summon visions and memories in the mind of the individual. Discernible order and coherence must still exist in music, because it is a form of communication, but through it, chaos may be summoned.

Proper black metal, if it is to be considered music and not merely a placeholder for an ideological or metaphysical concept, will display intelligibility for humans, however buried.

Variations lying and moving within iterations of fractals give us that impression of organic growth and dissolution. Black metal music accomplishes its replication of the natural flow — which is never in perfect balance, for that would represent stasis and utter death — through both imperfections in performance, divergences in expression of each instance, as well as an unconventional liberty in terms of structural strategy that takes it through multiform arrangements that correspond to the artist's inner state.

Imperfection in the performance of black metal places it in a sphere closer to folk music, and arises consciously as part of the ideology of artists who want to create something that places emotion and expression within a logical structure; this logical structure, furthermore, shapes itself to the needs of the music rather than usurping its leading character. In short, in black metal we find an expression of life beyond notions of good and evil, beautiful as well as dangerous, painful as well as torturously pleasurable.

Spirit in the Melody

TRADITIONALLY, WE SEE melody as the main aspect of music of the most primitive type. Here, melody and the motifs it develops dominate the direction of the content in the music as well as determine the quality and richness of the material. Textures, expressions and simple harmonies, then, come as supportive or auxiliary elements that enhance and complement the melody that lies at the very heart of the music. If one were to remove all but that central melody, a proper black metal song would still be easily recognizable.

Being modal, black metal may indulge in certain intervals that assert its motifs, but it is the overall arc described by the central tones within each riff and section that make clear a direction and narrative throughout a song. In a modal pattern, a melody will generally have a tone that serves as an anchor or pivot point (fulcrum); if it lacks this for whatever reason, then it is seriously crippled as a unit of information. These anchor points define the centre of each section, while the amplitude of the notes, that is the range throughout which they spread upwards or downwards, adds to the weight and sense of space. The quantity and speed of the notes may provide for a manner of intensity and momentum.

All of these factors conspire to bring the melody to life and possibly provide it with a distinctive personality which may or may not prove to be appropriate. A firm warning is in order at this point, that the reader does not therefore assume that we are implying that we can simply reduce the art to a mere straightforward, systematic arrangement of notes. These are, to be sure, observations on mechanics, but they are to be seen and appreciated as the material manifestations of a coherent mind, and as such only the effects of higher processes, and which effects go beyond the simple mechanics describes and involve a much more complex aural effect than can be easily and accurately described in words.

Judgement and perception, in the proper sense, of melodies in their contexts is an ability that is only honed through experience, insight, intuition and reason. Also crucial to its description is the term 'aural', which points out its wordless nature. It is occult because it speaks of a sense that cannot be directly made manifest but only apprehended through the bringing together and stepping beyond of the characteristics of music both measurable and otherwise.

The spirit of which we speak arises from the vibration of the physical particles when the notes are played; it is not the definition nor its description, but the sequence of logical, succeeding steps which invoke something that is very much alive and which may very well infect our being. While not embodied, it may attach itself to our own sequence of thoughts, giving rise to new patterns, evoking memories and feelings in the host.

The daemon that is born from the melody interacts with each consciousness in much the same way as a mathematical function that maps an input to an output. The input is whatever material our minds already contain and our own inherent power of drawing relations. The output spreads new patterns in the mind, creating new pathways. Thus, akin to demonic possession, the gradual descent of an open mind down the spiralling staircase and into the unknown, effects a very real change. The manner and extent of this change moreover, is dictated by the capacity and vulnerability of the listener; which vulnerability is sometimes willingness and thus a conscious, unspoken agreement to be transformed by these spirits.

Black metal percussion

BEING PRIMARILY BASED on the sound of the electric guitar, metal music faces a limitation in that it cannot vary dynamics in the traditional way by allowing differences in attack and hand-feel to have pronounced effects on the volume, though a degree of nuance in texture and quality can, in fact, result from such manipulations; this impediment seems to negate a whole dimension of music that is responsible for making it feel alive.

Black metal developed a solution to this problem in a rather interesting manner: percussion was taken to its textural extremes without relinquishing its traditional functions. Percussion simultaneously became subordinate to the needs of the whole, while at the same time achieving greater freedom of exploration for itself and other elements of the music as their freedom was ascertained. That is, the percussive section became a whole layer unto itself which would counterpoint and correspond with the rest of the layers instead of simply serving to emphasize or mark time.

On the one hand, in becoming first and foremost a constant textural background, percussion allowed the riff itself to be liberated to wander around melodically without losing the propelling motion that this kind of music needed. On the other, by simplifying and focusing the basic role of percussion, drummers became free to choose a wider variety of choices in how to produce the beat, thus opening up a world of possibilities when it came to textures and patterns.

The implication of the latter was that the background could take many different shapes and intensities, the variation of which would have a very strong impact on the whole, effectively becoming a modifier of dynamics by a sheer modulation of beat intensity and timbre. The result is that black metal becomes free to explore limits in both melodiousness and aggression that were previously out of bounds for existing forms of metal still dependent on the conventions of rock music percussion.

Once again, the esoteric labyrinth presented by black metal, this time at the level of percussion, serves multiple functions; at the sensual level, the immediate apprehension, it must transmit the sensation of raw, existential feeling that comes from a living on the edge or being in a life-threatening situation where the now is what matters most and everything else resides to the background so that only what is truly most essential and honest remains. Besides the feeling of impending danger, the percussion must unite with the rest of the music in inducing atrance of particularly dark character that is beyond introspective and of a rather a-personal nature. It is not the most fanciful or recondite of techniques that brings about the desired result, but the precise and nuanced application of clear expressions that together form intelligible recounts in the form of music.

Percussion serves the important role of controlling dynamics in a music where the main melodic instrument is capable of very little of it in terms of volume. And in utilizing the density of patterns and different timber of the drums as this intensity and volume regulator, it is possible to achieve modulation without losing a sense of power or the sense of alternating tension and unleashing in the unforgiving manner that the is required. A drummer's choice of a particular pattern, and whatwe would consider adornments in ride and cymbal overlaid patterns, adjusts the flow of energy in the piece significantly; this is the soul vehicle of the work as a living being.

Episodic Progression

BLACK METAL TENDS TO structure its raw compositions without a clear template; however, there is a certain methodological proclivity which, although perhaps unspoken, gives rise to a story-telling within the music. The narrative aspect of black metal can take many forms, but it can be presumed that all proper black metal must develop it in one way or another; it may be that long stretches of repetition aiming to reach an emotional and spiritual plateau produce this effect as they are laid out in a particular sequence, or it may take on a more explicitly progressive form in trying to produce variations on motifs and directed changes of expression in a clear articulation of coherent moods.

Black metal aims to reach beyond first impressions and into settled, long-term states that allow the listener to sink into himself, perhaps even stopping or slowing down the infinitely minute sequences of dazzling pictures that make up our immediate perception of reality. The process of those who would find pathways in the appropriate music requires of them the will to move forward, the will to let go, and the faculty of intuition that renders the soul a malleable but firm material able to react; but it must also be possessed of the power to execute its own decisions, that it may explore depths and discover secrets of all kinds, rather than be simply swept along the current.

Plateaus of aural landscapes designed to summon dark archetypes will progress in an order through which one will sense change within rather constant textures. The reader must nonetheless understand these observations as necessarily open descriptions of what knowledgeable and sensitive listeners have condensed irrespective of the opinions of the masses and less stable minds. No pretence of law or rule, but a retrospective and functional observation of what remains constant among the greatest of black metal works.

Textures and Intrinsic Meanings

BEING OF A PREDOMINANTLY homophonic texture and having developed its approach to percussion to the point of being able to relieve it from its traditional rock-music duties in a way that greatly resembles and is undeniably inspired by electronic music, black metal's textural changes become more important than anything else. Maintaining proper control of the ways changes are introduced, the time during which they are preserved and the order in which episodes occur become the greatest preoccupation of the talented black metal artist.

The character of each riff and its accompaniment by percussion go hand in hand when it comes to matters of arrangement; and lesser black metal music may be distinguished for its overt disavowal of these observations. Herein lies the trap of black metal: as it is traditionally based on extremely minimalist components, it is then thought, by some, to be easily subject to improvements through sheer and vulgar addition of note quantity and contrasts of expression and character; such a confusion, moreover, finds its origin in two misapprehensions typical of egotist minds.

The first is thinking that their emotional reaction to music is enough evaluation of the quality of art. The second is an utter obliviousness regarding the relation between human perceptions of structures and the patterns within music that give rise to a consistent set of complex laws; these laws cannot be interpreted linearly, but must rather be analysed in parallel. Such laws regarding the sound textures, moreover, play a similar role to that of the aural and cultural communication that takes place amongst humans and which goes beyond mere grammatical definitions, but which communication nonetheless remains inextricably linked with certain definitions and choices of words, so to speak.

It is clear that all melodies played on a single string without distortion will differ in the impression they make from those plucked with distortion; and that there is a considerable difference between the effects and impressions when each of these are simply plucked and allowed to ring, or when they are singly strummed with that fluttering technique commonly known as tremolo picking. As the effect of each of these is taken into serious consideration and tested aurally to identify and sense their unique effects arising from being applied to a kind melody or pattern, each of which could display wide range of distinct characteristics, one becomes aware of the rich well of possible messages and atmospheres which can be conveyed through their arrangement.

Furthermore, and as the vibrancy and intensity is held in nuanced regard, we may realise what a delicate operation each choice in construction is. In this light, haphazard and overly eager transitions and juxtapositions in the kind of music that tends to be careless and carefree now reveal a lack of depth, perhaps even a spiritual negligence in disregarding holistic effects, or a perilous ignorance at the very least.

In alliance with considerations regarding the potency of different techniques or particular patterns is the time through which each phrase or section is allowed to extend and loop. The overall balance of all these factors must be considered, and the failure of a single one of them usually induces a crippling effect that becomes apparent to the sense given enough time and openness of the mind to its perception. That is to say, even if we do not yet hold the keys to a detailed conscious understanding of the connection between music structure and effect, or even if are never destined to receive such knowledge, being aware of it and working in accordance to its reality is the only way to transcendence and beyond: evolution.

TOWARDS A SINISTER FUTURE

THE IDEAS OUTLINED throughout this essay give us a hint of what black metal could become, that a power that has hitherto lain dormant may yet serve to propel individuals ascribing to it as transcendental art in ways that direct and define a future elite culture. The proposed angle of transcendental, dark alchemy that exists within strands of black metal can go well beyond the merely obfuscating, staged persona creation that has become the fetish of so many self-avowed pseudo-Satanists. Not only is such posturing completely relegated to contingency, but in its unwitting deception, it misleads many of those with dark musical potential, yet unfamiliar with this musical art, to the impression that the poseur's aesthetic presentation is the core.

That the intent is to scrape such exoteric staging, and instead move towards an honest esoteric apprehension should be perfectly clear by now. For in aligning the movement with all that is efficacious instead of what merely gratifies the senses, to unite faculties towards an understanding rather than falling into dogmatic intransigence, and taking the road of action through excellence in the breaking of boundaries the dark art can serve as a medium to the totality of reality —or as much of it as we are able to take in.

Examining the past, we may observe that the greatest works came about from a desire to open doors, to let an acausal stream of energy suffuse the area where the air itself would be disrupted by the vibration patterns arranged to that end; in them we do not hear the artist speaking, but his lending of personal talents as a tool for an a-personal manifestation to take place.

To think that a majority would embrace the difficult path that leads to transcendent creation and immortality, would be naive, to say the least. One would have to speak of a Transcendent Black Metal; for such a distinction to become real the art by which adherents etch out these rituals would have to be weighed on its own merit; in so doing, we would be setting an impasse that would obstruct the way for all mediocre artistic works.

The intention is not to detract from any personal reputation, honour, or earned merit, but to let artistic merit be also earned as per a just and holistic weighing of the work in itself. That is, elitism is extended from a valuation of intellect and ideological stance to artistic creation, so that the art-form itself, and not merely the intent behind it, may be ennobled intrinsically, as it were, from within.

One must remember that European musical tradition followed a constructive path of discovery, where experimentation did not imply the disavowal of what had been built until that moment, but struggled in the creation of a repository of discovered knowledge. Until now, aversion towards musical tradition had its origin in a grave misapprehension of where the value of a tradition is located and how it may feed growth rather than stunt it.

Growth would be possible that would preserve an essence in transformation across time, especially if it were to become a true aural tradition. A similar phenomenon seemed to manifest itself in the analogue tape trading community that wilfully maintained an underground status. Its spiralling into superficial collectionism is only one more way in which we see how underground black-death's great potential for mythos, and so a magickal channelling, was for the most part squandered by a lack of proper tending.

Lower intellects have been unable to separate concrete form from abstracted pattern, a confusion that has bled into the cracks of a largely unconscious culture. Learning from Tradition, correctly apprehended, would lead to a depth in understanding and practice of the nature of organized sound, which would in turn lead black metal to richer material planes; enough emphasis cannot be placed on the idea that such a learning and subsequent application cannot, if it is to have any value of its own, consist of an imitation of idiosyncratic elements in the older music; black metal must always remain, in essence, what it is: ever becoming yet never losing itself.

Stagnancy is never an option for something that is alive, and to be alive is to be in constant change and transformation. For black metal to remain what it is, it must remain connected to its bloody muse at all levels; it must cause throw one into lacerating introspection, and a horrific presentiment of life unto death, pleasure unto pain. Music itself must, furthermore, be conducive to a natural intellectual cultivation, and as such is intrinsically elitist in that such an apprehension cannot be taught but must be developed by the individual possessed of a latent ability. The purposeful cultivation of abilities should greatly aid in the bringing about of a fuller and faster development of those individuals who already possess the seed which may or may not blossom and grow into stout mastery.

A SORCEROUS CRAFT

Fluxions

In his quest for accuracy and rigour eventually leading to his contributions to Calculus, Sir Isaac Newton borrowed terminology from an area of classical mechanics called Kinematics. The terms fluent and fluxion incorporated eventually came to be known as variable and derivative. Each set of terms has its advantages in describing the object in question, highlighting one or another aspect. Fluxion in particular is quite useful in poetically illustrating an 'instantaneous rate of change,' and may serve us outside the realm of pure mathematical abstraction to bring attention to such immediate movement at each point in time. So, while the change from a measure to the next, from an idea to the next are changes in fluents, there can be said to exist fluxions in music which describe movements across a separate dimension —that of the inner experience. But such a transposition into the realm of musical description is only metaphorical, if useful to expand perception, and should be taken as a flexible mental aid.

Metal can be reduced to musical phrases, around which percussive patterns of different timbres and complimentary effects are added. In its most natural state, divested of rock and blues voicings, metal music is monophonic. Many bands from the original underground throughout the eighties, constructed monophonic textures consisting of a guitar and bass playing the same notes, differing in any case by an octave, and only carefully and sparingly resorting to a separation of a fifth between the instruments. The other most common technique along this narrow bridge to the expression of power is the organum, albeit used in its most simplified form only, allowing for a sense of space and relative movement while limiting any weakening effects over the main phrasal line.

Metal inherited the guitar riff from rock n' roll music, which had in turn received it from blues music. Phrases were already present in blues, but as short rhythmic bits that cycled ostinatostyle under the characteristic explosiveness of African vocalizations. The riff passed on to rock music, which dilutes the powerful and raw effects of the blues riff. It brings these effects under the umbrella of ready-made chord-cycle recipes over which a melody line is highlighted, and which melody line is the true centre of rock music. The hard blues rock of Jimmy Hendrix brought back the crudeness, & informed hard rock, as well as the earliest proto-meta, on the folk use of the guitar-riff. Black Sabbath finally took the riff and turned it into a technique in the service of a longer, more expressive phrase with echoes horror music soundtracks.

From the early phrasal music of Black Sabbath and its revival in eighties underground music we can see how the guitar-riff, in its phrase-oriented usage, can be made to create textures that create both ambience and decisive movement beyond melodic-harmonic distinctions by focusing on its modal aspect. It can be said that when metal attempts to break into the melodic-harmonic paradigm of mature European classical music, the power of the guitar-riff is taken away, quickly dragging down metal into a mediocre form excelling at nothing. The strength of metal music lies in preserving the integrity and power of the phrasal-riff through strict commitment to balance among an overall monophonic texture, a sensible use of organum, sensible use of doubling ('harmonizing') and an extremely measured use of polyphonic techniques. Introduced through the medium of the phrasal guitar-riff, the movements, motif-relations and motif-variations wield an immense power.

Less obvious is the discovery that the essence, and hence potential, of metal lies beyond the guitar-riff or the phrase in itself. That is, the inner experience which metal phrases induce in themselves and in sequence is connected to a sense of both movement and permanence, relative change through immanence —change not only through time but in-time— the universe in a drop of water, eternity in an instant. This is the black fluxion that is active within and throughout albums such as Hvis Lyset Tar Oss and Transilvanian Hunger, eluding as they do all concrete analysis against them but also in their favour — the bulk of which remain poetical allusions. The creation of fluxions appears to involve the testing and careful development of phrasal guitar-riffs. Effectual bringing about of the appropriate fluxion needs the clearest self-honesty of the artist regarding the rise of their inner experience and its circuitlike reflection with the musical passage created. The rediscovery of said fluxions lies beyond the first threshold of experience of the corresponding phrasal guitar-riffs, and many listeners are able to sense them while remaining unable to verbalize their experience because of the lack of an abstract and theoretical framework the terms of which can be referenced.

Against first appearances, we are not entirely contradicting the non-referentialist position. The idea of the centrality of a fluxion in the metal dynamic pertains the fact that there is an element of living (as opposed to dead, static, or reduced) music that involves the inner experience in-time. The inclusion of the inner experience within a rational discussion on music aesthetics may appear to revive an empty metaphysical tendency to cite objects and events beyond perception or description, but rest assured that this is not the case at the

present. The fluxion in question is specifically the perception of a rent opening, a space created, a movement realized, by the phrasal guitar-riff as a unit. Furthermore, this helps us come to the realization that historically, and in essence, metal music moves towards pieces composed of 'flows'. Reductions of the music in metal analyses to 'riffs' or simply 'phrases', while well-founded, are always unable to approach the aforementioned essence. The concept of fluxions and their role in the concept of a music consisting of flows may provide the abstract basis for a more encompassing understanding.

Anton Long's Fluxions of Time and Alchemical Seasons Applied

IN A HIGHLY RELEVANT essay titled Alchemical Seasons and the Fluxions of Time, Anton Long lists a set of postulates concerning the concepts spelled out in the title. The idea stems from a certain time-relativistic point of view deriving from the theory of causal and acausal universes, if one wills, though one may also imagine they are different sets of dimensions in the existing universe we know. In one way, the implication is that every single thing follows its own pace, developing according to its nature and, in the case of living beings, in symbiosis with the acausal intrusion they allow as gateways.

We will proceed to take from the postulates that concern our concise and direct presentation of metal riffs viewed as fluxions, but the reader is encouraged to study the pertinent text in full. It should be clear that these extemporizations on the original themes are to be taken as creative explorations of concepts that may or may not yield a logical extension of the ontology, but which are primarily aimed at reinforcing a conscious understanding of organic, intuitive, processes that could (and probably have been) brought under sorcerous activity.

The following discussions use ample use of the Greek word φύσις, transliterated as phusis by Martin Heidegger, and as physis by Anton Long. A recommended text to be properly introduced to this concept in a modern philosophic treatment, we may recommend Heidegger's Introduction to Metaphysics. The following is the philosopher's basic statement regarding the term phusis in page 15:

"Now what does the word phusis say? It says what emerges from itself (for example, the emergence, the blossoming, of a rose), the unfolding that opens itself up, the coming-intoappearance in such unfolding, and holding itself and persisting in appearance—in short, the emerging-abiding sway."

We will hereafter transliterate physis as per Anton Long, whose text we will be discussing.

In the third postulate of his essay Alchemical Seasons and the Fluxions of Time, Anton Long writes:

"Time is a Fluxion. That is, time is already inherent in living beings, part of their physis."

From which follows that if what is contained concealed, in metal riffs are fluxions, it means that these are to find their source in the artist / performer / guitarist themselves as living beings. It emanates from them, with the impediment being their incapacity at the instrument on the one hand, or an encumbering analytical consciousness of what is coming forth. Furthermore, the technical ability distorts or changes the presentation of the emanated physis of the music as fluxion, though in no definitive way. That is, a higher dexterity or dominion in the technical field does not necessarily result in greater clarity or purity in the expression of the art, and may indeed be the cause of obfuscation or artificial embellishment, where 'artificial' refers to a conscious construction not necessarily directly guided by that inner flow beyond the individual as a gate to the acausal.

Following from the previous, we read:

"Each living being has a Fluxion appropriate to – which represents/manifests/presences – its physis and thus which is appropriate to/manifests its type/species of life."

The implication here is not a revelation in regards to art, when we modify this to refer to the birth of metal riff-phrases emanating from the individual. The resulting music is an expression of what that person is, rather than simply what they want to say, the latter being the most popular conception. In short, in exposing their art, the artist reveals a part of themselves in a particular state. What is interpreted thereof by an audience or critic is the subject matter of a different discussion. Also, what is interpreted about the method as a causal expression more or less conducive and appropriate to communication is different from a judgement on the fluxion, and thus on the individual's physis itself. The latter is moralistic, while the former is pertains the craft of musicmaking as an intelligible medium.

Then,

"Thus, linear time - as measured by a fixed causal calendar and/or as defined by such things as the ratio of distance and velocity of a physical object – is Appearance/Abstraction not Reality."

In relation to the analysis of music, we may take this to mean that the individual physis is reflected upon the art, the music, independently of points of view, of nurturing culture, or even of training. Also, that this expression of the fluxion comes out at the pace appropriate and commensurate to the physis of the artist.

A gross distortion of the previous point might have been interpreted as if the determination of the 'correctness' of music, whether it be by its orderliness or its adherence to a certain narrative expectation, are simply illusions, and that the essence of it lies somewhere in a space entirely inaccessible to consciousness out of touch with some gnostic revelation or trance. But such would have been a misapprehension of what the original postulate refers to, as they specifically pertain to constraining the riff-phrase fluxion to a speed of unveiling or development, and to the notion of points of view being only apparent to the one reality of what the fluxion is as part and parcel of physis.

Consequently,

"Such linear time thus re-presents only the causal physis/ nature of material objects/matter and thus manifests the physis/nature of the causal."

That is, whatever part of the riff-phrase in question that is measured with respect to its quantifiable ratios is not that ulterior intrusion from the acausal that we are expecting from the artist as gateway, but only a gross, materialist, causal attempt to somehow measure it. This we may perhaps even apply to the repetitiousness of a riff-phrase.

And so,

"A Fluxion manifests what is a-causal. That is, how a particular living being changes/develops/manifests."

The riff-phrase as a fluxion of the artist's physis is reflecting of 'how' that person is, rather than 'what' they are.

From this last point, we may take that the artist can only express what manifests through him, as something they have absorbed, made their own, and brought forth again. That is, the individual as a result of a cosmic collocation of intermediary stellar generator agents, and not the ultimate essence that perhaps is a thread beyond the initial cause and into the preternatural void. Consequently, whatever he will express authentically, he must first invoke, embody from within and through actions flowing because they are necessary to the individual, and thus, temporarily become by unveiling.

Possession

ESCHEWING THE DISCUSSION of whence the different phenomena which have throughout history been identified as possession, whether they are psychological, physiological or paranormal in origin, we are interested here only in the effects of such altered states. More specifically, we are concerned with the use of the possessed state of mind as a way to enter into a space where communication is made possible in a way that facilitates the by-passing of the rational, judging mind, by opening a back door, through which non-discursive information can be passed between artist and audience. This implies two things: that the artist must be possessed during the birth of the work, and that the audience must be possessed as well at the moment of reception. The latter may be accomplished either through independent preparation, or by the work of art, in this case music, inducing such a state by purposeful design.

It may be posited that this leads to true expression, as opposed to mere exercise, invention or imitation. In order to justify such a claim within our currently developing framework, let it be noted that in the state of possession, by definition, something beyond the individual interacts with him. By way of explanation, we are saying that during possession there is a coincidence of the human mind and whatever entities or force inhabit such acausal spaces beyond our own causal one. It remains unclear whether the artist thus operating also injects something of his own individuality into such spaces, so that music is a function of a commingling. A more enticing, because more inclusive of other observations and explanations, is that humans acts only as gates which, once opened or activated, suppose a passageway between acausal and causal spaces. The implication might then be that what we identify as individuality is simply the effect of the unique location of the human being upon an interdimensional topography where specific acausal forces irrupts into a particular causal point.

In the first part of his book Understanding Music Philosophy, Roger Scruton writes,

"We must see music as an act of communication, which crucially depends upon placing within the listener's first person perspective a state of mind that is not his own."

He arrives at his conclusion as a synthetic addition to a logical cascade culminating with a correction, an expansion, of Wittgenstein's comments on music and the first-person perspective. The tacit crux of the matter is that this communication can only be effected from the inside of mind, of being, without core, non-discursive information being deformed by the parsing of the filters that enter into action in perspectives other than the solitary, inward-looking one.

Scruton paves the way by identifying what he calls the acousmatic experience of listening to sounds, whereby they are perceived as "animated by a continuous movement". As he tirelessly makes it known to us, no such continuity is physically extant in the sequence of tones that make up music, which more often than not can be described as discrete events. We may add here that while training and conditioning can facilitate a number of types of perception, it is most likely that the capacity for acousmatic perception is inherent in human beings as a species, and which capacity most likely gave rise to music as a form of communication as well as an art form —and certainly not the other way around.

Scruton continues to elaborate by describing the quasisemantic structure that can be perceived in music, and which the reader may interpret as a direct consequence of the aforementioned acousmatic experience. Now, not only do we hear continuity, but discursive significance. Scruton at least implies a comparison to narrative by his choice of the term semantic. However, we may venture to replace the narrative interpretation with a more flexible, abstract one that sees not grammar, punctuation marks and story-telling, but nondiscursive events that do not necessarily align with a linear cause and effect sequence.

Having entered a state of possession, what sounds and images are produced should not merely appear as something else, nor should they be defined by how different from other things they sound. It is not in appearing to be one thing or another that music acquires value, nor is possession itself an immediate voucher for value, depending on what one is looking for. What possession enables is the communication of analogous states of mind that may be experienced by the artist. What exactly this artist opens, and transmits are a function of what that person is and accomplishes causally, and what that opens acausally. That is to say, the ability, or the experience of an artist in being possessed, as it were, does not confer upon them anything beyond the ability in itself, as a worthless being might only be a gateway to rubbish, however ethereal that rubbish would be in essence.

Mesmerism

HAVING ESTABLISHED the way in which the artist may access a state of mind that allows for a communication beyond the daytime ego, as well as the ways in which what is musically discovered and produced while in that state can be perceived as having clear vectors of force, the next step entails the efficient delivery of experience to an audience. Now, Music is based in the capacity of human beings to perceive it through an acousmatic experience, and thereby sensuously, and inwardly, feel the movement of fluxions, more profoundly even than what could be described as a narrative. The latter presupposes a certain degree of familiarity with the forms, so that there may be barriers that require a certain acclimatization period to the sonic affront first of all, but also to the inducement of pain on humane sensibilities. After this has been accomplished, the individual in the audience may become the receptor of the acausal disruption potentially to be enacted by his giving in to the fluxions of the music. To that end, the musician can design the music structure so that it facilitates this process further, organizing the passages so that the fluxions therein act in collaboration with each other beyond technique, and rather in an organic discovery that assembles them together.

First is a stage of preparation, in which the listener is presented with something utterly intelligible, which communicates something that is known to the listener, in one way or another. It does not follow that the presentation, the idea, or the introduction, whatever name one chooses to give it, should be something derivative or mediocre. It is intelligibility, perhaps expressed in clarity, and good simplicity. At this stage, we are trying to bypass the defences, the prejudice and calculation, of the receptor. And so, disarmament of objections and judgements should be first carried out. Compounded with the aforementioned disarmament by the exposition to not necessarily safe, but identifiable queues, is the effect of luring in, whereby we have active listeners that may "walk into" the fog on their own, as it were. For this to succeed, familiarity is not enough since interest must be aroused to the point of desire.

Once the listener's conscious attention, his willingness to cooperate, to allow himself to be lead somewhere, has been secured, the music may proceed to a step that Milton H. Ericksson has called induction in his book Hypnotic Realities. Induction entails helping the conscious to relinquish dominance, so that communication with the unconscious, which in any case always takes place, can occur without interruptions and objections. Ideally, we want to induce a trance, by which we do not mean that any kind of overt outward symptoms would have to be necessarily visible. It simply moves the conscious portion of the mind into a kind of automatic mode in which some direct control is relinquished to the unconscious. Our efforts to do this must flow from the previous stage of familiarization and luring in, that we may send away the conscious mind into its own reverie within an individual realm of phantasia that is now being sustained by the music.

The listener is not merely sent into any trance, but into a trance in the direction of the musician's election, though within the constraints that each individual in the audience will allow, giving the latter a handle over what can possibly occur next.

Once the subject has been entranced, development and complexity are given their rightful place, but at first with the explicit aim of deepening the current state of mind. The musician strives to crystallize an aural vision of a world down the path that the listener at first took consciously, and which then grew of its own accord. The purpose of this step is to entirely bind the receptor, to effectively bring them into a different reality from which what they normally understand as reality appears simply as a perspective, or a distant land they once inhabited but have left far behind in lieu of more wondrous possibilities, however dark these may appear at first, for they are also immensely pleasurable even when they bring copious amounts of pain.

Finally, the crucial matter can be transformed into melodies and structures that are to be unleashed upon the subject. Here is where suggestion takes place, where evocation takes place in earnest by planting seeds that will later grow of their own accord. Here where the most powerful, insidious, and more difficult to comprehend passages can be exposed, though not without careful consideration. The mind is now open for invasion by a contaminant that will soak its ground. To fully take advantage, musical fluxions of the most jarring find place in the shape of climaxes, the full building of which entail not just the progression of previous stages, but an ascent of its own. This way, it attains independent personality and weight, though care must be taken not to divorce it from the previous material, which would suppose a disruption of the kosmos already created.

Once satisfied with the work done, the listener should be led away, outside from this particular phantasia which must remain sacred, even if forgotten, and should not be approached nonchalantly, which would, if not void, at least undermine the integrity of the contents communicated. This outro, so to call it, is a controlled resurfacing or exiting, which must be firm but also reassuring of what has previously occurred, concentrating on driving stability.

Dure and Sedue

FROM THE CHANNELLING forth of acausally inspired, motivated fluxions manifest as riff-phrases through spells of invocation or even possession, we moved towards their conscious, calculated arrangement in accordance to the Ericksonian style of mesmerism. The third stage in the exposition of the sorcerous sonic art is its performance, by which is not necessarily meant the performance in front of an audience, and includes its performance at the time of recording as a definitive impression upon the chosen media. It is clear that what at this point is most important is how to achieve the best possible performance that the already arranged expressions for the fluxions' manifestations can be communicated to the receivers, the audience.

In an article titled Ritual Magick - Dure and Sedue Ceremonial, the obscured contributor to the Order of Nine Angles collection Hostia makes the following distinction:

"Basically, there are two types of ceremonial workings in magick: dure ceremonial, and sedue ceremonial. The first is essentially ritual used for internal magick – to produce/provoke/inspire changes within the consciousness of those participating/attending. The second is (or rather should be) a performance which transports the individual participants to another realm and which engages their whole being.(...) A ceremonial ritual is a seduction – of the participants/congregation by he/she/they conducting it or the power of the rite itself because the rite captures or transforms an aspect or aspects of the acausal. This seduction is subtle if the ritual is a sedue one, and obvious/overt/harsh if it is a dure one."

The latter concerns participants in a theatrical ceremonial setting, while the former matches the purposes of communicating through inner change, by becoming internal magick. The recording or performance of the fluxion-suffused arrangements approached this way becomes a conscious, measured, sober yet highly involved effort at crafting real sonic sorcery.

Drawing attention to the nature of the dure ceremonial, that it is used for internal magick, implies active participation on the part of the audience. In the case of music, it necessarily means that the sorcery in question will not be effective without the audience not simply 'listening' to the music as it plays in the background or through a cynic's rationalizing filter, but rather welcoming it as a swaying to and fro of the total experience.

The total experience being firstly the perception of the raw sound 'materials', whether their abrasiveness or their smoothness; secondly, the directly resulting emotions from any source, be that the acousmatic experience of an imaginary flow through space, or the emotional processing of the raw materials; thirdly, the rational perception that encompasses appreciation for structure, as well as narrative and extra-musical elaborations and interpretations; and lastly, the incipientalterations in willpower and willingness towards courses of action, seeds which, if watered and tended, flower into new states of being and the possibility of a further unveiling of the individual physis.

ARS SYMPHONICA

Poison from the Abyss: A commentary after Ebvleb's Poizon of god

I

In giving birth and nurturing Abyssum's second great work, Ebvleb became keen on a mystical concept he termed the poison of god, a name with which he baptized the musical work itself. At first glance, it might seem apparent that there is an antireligious posture implicit in this name, and while this is true to some extent insofar as Abyssum is opposed to organized cults and the god mythos as a whole, the nature of the work under discussion is strictly mystical.

A closer knowledge of the materials should suggest to those with sufficient intellectual power that there is a more nuanced interpretation to be found, and which interpretation necessitates an apprehension of Abyssum as dark and sinister mysticism channelling forces from a different dimension — from the acausal universe. Brett Stevens has provided a more nuanced interpretation of the codification of Ebvleb's mystic exposition of what this poison is. Correctly understood, the poison in question is not a substance concocted for the demise of god, its existence not being recognized in the first place. Instead, the words of Ebvleb reveal a double meaning: our poisoning by the lies of the god mythos turns those rare, superior minds possessed of reason to become hardened against the delusions that hold the common man of simian mind in their grasp; in turn, those thus changed become a poison for a society based on illusions and mediocrity.

Abyssum, as representation of the forces driving it, is then said to be a poison for all that is mundane, but as a poison it is at once lethal to unworthy minds incapable of its proper handling but an elixir of liberation to a very few who may in time become one with it. We may understand Abyssum's mystical conceptualization as the condensation of two different substances into a single symbolic term: the poison of lies and delusion, and a cleansed poison that is itself an antidote to them. What separates them, what brings forth the second substance, is the filter through which the initial poison is distilled, and which filter is a particular human essence unique to each individual.

II

IN HIS WORK THE WILL to Power, Nietzsche refers to Christianity as a poisonous substance that breaks the strong, dissuading them from their natural tendency to courageous action and replacing pride with constant doubt to the point of sickness. We find in these words a description of Ebvleb's first poison, received from a sick and deluded humankind. The German armchair thinker steps further and states that ideals are poisonous because they distort what is real. He admits, however, that ideals are indispensable as temporary measures.

To understand the full depth of Nietzsche's words, one can see them in light of the dark elitism of Abyssum. Nietzsche was a philosopher that insisted on a nobility of the mind, of reason, rather than one of birth. He also favoured the idea that most people are simply incapable of understanding, a thought that permeated and defined the way in which he graciously expressed himself, uncaring and dismissive of having to justify himself in ways that contemporary intellectuals could understand, not to speak of the common rabble.

Given these and other observations regarding Nietzsche's exposition of the excellence of the superior man on the one hand, and the mediocrity and incompetence of the majority on the other, the perspicacious reader may see that Nietzsche does not mean to do away with ideals or values. Nietzsche tells us that these are as dangerous as poison can be, yet they are also a necessary antidote to be utilized in a certain way.

III

A FURTHER UNVEILING can be sought behind Nietzsche's reference to Plato as the destroyer of paganism. Plato is paralleled with moral fanaticism, and is accused by the German of poisoning the innocence of paganism by a re-evaluation of its values. Here, we must go beyond the prejudiced intellectualism of Nietzsche and dismiss his misrepresentation of Plato as a moral fanatic.

We should agree that Plato was indeed the evil of which Swedenborg spoke as the poison of the serpent, antagonistic to innocence. Upon inspection, the origin of the word evil reveals something interesting. It resides in the Gothic ubils, which implies beyond and going beyond due limits. In evil is the excellence of the strong, of those possessed of discernment and courage.

It is only with discernment that we can look beyond the materialistic understanding of the Myth of the Cave as dualism, and which discernment alone can take us beyond mere words and reconcile Plato's idea with a transcendental monism that sees the universe as one whole in which opposites are correspondences with a common origin. Thus through monism is the Judaic idea of the good god poisoned beyond salvation,and the infernal torment of living correctly understood as a delight in strife and overcoming. Innocence is the mark of animals and brutes; superior man is a demon of transgression.

IV

AN ALLEGORICAL COUNTERPART to the Poison of god may be found in the mystical understanding that European Tradition has regarding the plant Henbane. Grimassi writes about Henbane, Hyoscyamus niger, that it is associated in magickal workings with the creation of barriers and fixing things in place, and thus to blocking, stopping activity and disrupting communication.

Henbane has a double effect as it disconnects the victim's perceptions of the physical world around him, while increasing internal bodily activity unto hallucination, delirium, heightened emotions and convulsion. It is a dangerous plant that estranges and kills most, but which in the hands of a few knowledgeable and daring individuals becomes an instrument that turns the eye, through delirium and trauma, towards the stars and away from this planet in its mundane aspect. Henbane is both a cure to ailments and a lethal poison, depending on usage.

In a short but valuable document titled Herbs in Black Magick, written by the Traditional Satanist Hagur, we find references to Henbane as having a powerful, oppressive and nauseous odour, and whose effects are hypnotic and convulsive. Hagur quotes Culpeper warning to the reader, to only use Henbane externally as ointment but never to ingest it. Such a warning can further illustrate the metaphysical Poison of god, which the average man can only appreciate superficially and is undeserving to ingest.

The raging depth in subtlety of the music and aura of Abyssum's Poizon of god could be described in a similar manner by those of us who have attempted to establish meditative and empathic connections with the work. One might note that Benedictus Crispus mentions Henbane not only under its well known name, Hyoscyamus, but also, more obscurely, Symphonica.

V

HAGUR ALSO IMPLIES how, in the Sinister Tradition, Henbane is connected to Saturn. Hagur helps support the validity of this connection by quoting the opinion of Culpeper, who states that an observation and inspection of Henbane in its natural environment and its effects should yield the conclusion that it is a Saturnine plant, rather than one connected with Jupiter, mocking contemporary astrologers for said confusion.

Among the incense blends mentioned by Hagur as appropriate for working on the planetary spheres of Hebdomadry, Henbane is also seen as common to the blends for Mercury and Saturn, exclusively. Mercury is individualized by the presence of Sulphur in its blend, while Saturn likewise acquires its character by the inclusion of Ash. Sulphur and Ash are considered traditional links to either of the two planets, and so Henbane could be said to be a catalyst to their interaction. It is worthy of commentary that the set of incenses to which this indication belongs corresponds to the Sulphur stage of Sphere Workings, which aim at the subtle perception of a more experienced practitioner (as in those glimpsed in MSS Hostia I, II, III).

In analysing the link between Mercury and Saturn in the Sinister Tradition, we are called to inspect the dark pathway and corresponding Dark God which embodies it: Abatu. The corresponding Sinister Atu image is XVI: The Tower, also formerly known as War. A passing mention could be made here that the Basque word abatu means to support a house, while in Latvian and Lithuanian, it is a noun-form of the word father, meaning a Catholic abbot. Now, both the conventional image and the Sinister image of this Atu imply the destruction of an edifice by lightning —a natural force, a Satanic presence descending in full force to behead the figurative abbot as a symbol of the materialistic cult of the Jewish god.

In the description of Sinister Atu XVI in the book Naos, there is mention of a woman in white standing at the gates of a castle whose tower is toppled by lightning. It is implied that she is working the magick that brings down the lightning upon the said edifice. A similar figure is found in Bram Stoker's The Lair of the White Worm, where a pale and seductive lady, who always dresses in white and who we intuit has a manner of mental powers, belongs to a family that possesses giant serpent-like monster. The monster is a white wyrm kept hidden underground by this family with ancient ties and an unmistakable sinister aura.

Lightning descending and a serpent ascending are both well-known symbols of illumination, and of Lucifer. But in relation to the more pure and Sinister work of Ebvleb, we should refer specifically to the Promethean Satan: the way of lonely and independent illumination through strife and suffering given only to a very few, perhaps those very few who alone are worthy of the Poison of god. This Poison from the Abyss is a portal through Mercury unto chaotic forces from beyond Saturn.

VI

THE AFOREMENTIONED derivations and systems all relate to the
Hellenic mysteries and to Alchemy. With this in mind, a few
pertinent references may be found in Alasdair Forsythe's
Alchemy Deciphered. The author quotes from Baro Urbigerus'
1690 Alchemical Tract, where Urbigerus talks about a
Philosophical Distillation that is the right Separation of
Mercurial Water from its purely poisonous substance, which is
useless to the Art itself. This distillation of originally poisonous
Mercurial Water is carried out successfully only by Adepts, or those on the way to becoming one. In other words, those with the knowledge, spiritual acumen and intellect to do so

will achieve this transcendental victory. The power of Will that only a few possess, or which only a few may kindle, are referred to as Fire that alone has the cleansing power to remove poison and stench.

In Alchemy, the first step in a spiritual purification, or what Hellenic Gnostic thought would identify as the beginning of the journey towards the realms beyond the stars, is called Calcination. Forsythe further refers to alchemical tractates which describe how this process causes a terrible stench, likely to be poisonous. Said process should therefore be carried out in an open space, away from people. Transposing exoteric instructions to an esoteric understanding of a mystical path, it becomes clear that what is required is utmost care and separation from other people, since the transformation process is volatile and conflictive

VII

THE ACEPHALIC MYSTIC, Von Sanngetall, writes in an article published on June 12, 2017 titled 'Look for the interior of Eorthe!' that Calcinatio is the process of Fire or Purification. His brief exposition is consistent with our own understanding of the inner fire that can distil value from dangerous poison itself, a process which in itself incurs in learning. Von Sanngetall goesfurther here and gives us a necessary condition for that Fire to become lit inside of us. He talks of the necessity of taking in the living water of the Greater and Unresolved Mysteries, a statement that could be interpreted simplistically as faith, but which most likely refers to the opening up of mystic sensibilities, which in turn may also make one receptive to a greater reality.

Von Sanngetall continues to explain that the resulting purifying fire detaches us from a mundane mentality and all that comes with it, including blind habits and ideologies that are merely functional but cannot give provide us a complete understanding. In this rejection, he says, we also do away with utilitarian, materialistic and anthropocentric views that plague modern civilization.

Thus we heed what Ebvleb once referred to as Thy CallBeyond the Stars, and which call we now can understand as intimately connected to The Poison of god. Stepping inwards through the seven spheres reunites us, completes us and makes us ready for the two final stages crossing the Abyss and towards the stars.

An Interview with Ebvleb

1. D.A.R.G.: Did growing up in a geographic region where Catholicism predominates somehow affect your thought and, therefore, your art?

Ebvleb: What truly affects me are the characteristics of the territory which I inhabit, and of which I am proud to enjoy day to day; this country has no reason to envy foreign landscapes. I have volcanoes, mountains, lakes, rivers, forests, 'coldness', and a brain which connects to this. There are some details missing here, like snow, but this is quickly forgotten when being enveloped by the dense fog of my country's plateau; the volcanoes which I now see every day show me their power and transmit occasional arrangements that crackle like natural explosions. Being in contact with the Earth and the cosmos, my mind not only transmits my thinking and my feeling; it transmits my discussion with what is called NATURE of the planet and of the universe as far as I can reach. Theology cannot go by the hand of intelligent persons.

2. D.A.R.G.: From your viewpoint, what is black metal's reason-to-be? Has the panorama changed in these twenty years in a way that, the conditions which made its birth possible being now extinct, it is no longer plausible as an ideological movement in action and philosophy?

Ebvleb: Time has marked the mutation, there is some melancholy and a great hate for the loss of those days... but the way I see the order of things this is normal, nobody could have expected that so much musical quality would not inspire new generations, and the empty space had to be filled with what the current would bring. The fault with the bands of the past is now being popular conformists in their majority; the market grew and they did not oppose it in the minimum; all those who complain were at the same time keeping zines and interviewing each other for their respective publications. There was no way of avoiding the popularization of the genre, it is only little poser boys to possess melancholy for something that was only a mirage.

This misstep by the "great bands" has motivated those of a more profound soul to find an interest in affairs of greater import and therefore there arises the occasional proposal imbued in some kind of occultism or obscurantism. I cannot say that there exists no ideology and/or philosophy because I would be denying my own existence, but I can say that common humans are a majority; there have always been, there always are, and there will always be more thinking human beings who will enter the superior labyrinths inside that which we call Black Metal.

Personally, I have lost interest in what happens in the socalled scene; I simply follow my musical and ideological experiment; I hope to occasionally encounter some musical piece that shakes me energetically, because dark and hidden music captivates me. I will continue to dig among demos hoping to know how to choose what can interest me;

otherwise, it will be allowed to pass into the hands of those with lower demands.

3. **D.A.R.G.**: Handling different musical projects at the same time, each with differing characters and exterior forms, what is the central axis, if there is one, around which all of them circle, to which they refer in your personal cosmogony? Or, are they enterprises disconnected from each other like mental experiments in completely separate dimensions?

Ebvleb: Everything circles around each idea, no project has leadership in anything since that is a human standard and this goes beyond that. I take each idea into experimentation and it becomes a spiritual matter, if it is necessary, or in a compositional, emotional matter. I have the tendency to keep in permanent experimentation certain projects specifically like Cruel, Abyssum, Nigromante; these are part of my personality and artistic spirit, although the others which I have created along the way have remained in final states or simply resting before a next musical composition.

Nigromante will continue to elaborate sonorous orgies for master minds and Abyssum will continue exploring violence and obscurantism, while C.R.U.E.L. comes for the horns of musical bestiality.

4. **D.A.R.G**: The nature of the purest art makes it inaccessible to those humans who exercise the grossest

thinking, and to those who some call homo hubris. This is why speaking of bands that should be famous but which were not lacks any real meaning for who seeks transcendental art. Could you give us a couple of examples of magnificent albums from the golden era of underground metal which were kept away from mundane hands and ears?

Ebvleb: I do have a few titles in mind, but they are DEMOS; the masterpieces were dispersed mercilessly, and rarities come out into the light in the present. But I can vouch for the fact that there still exists a fine layer of recordings in cassette that are not obtainable even when excavating in the graves of the creators themselves; these recordings of which I have some, I would never mention in a magazine or in public; but if there was an opportunity to visit my sewer and, among the calls of the night, invade thought with these recordings which in my opinion are jewels of BLACKMETAL.

5. D.A.R.G.: So-called scenes are usually an excuse for aiding mutual delusion; however, when these are the natural result of honest ideological and spiritual brotherhoods, they reflect a sense of purpose which crystalizes in unique works of art of great power, these having been emanations from beyond normal human consciousness.

Ebvleb: : I have nothing to say on this matter; I care little about belonging to something; I am independent in every sense and I intend to continue being so: a black point within the black, an underground within another underground hides me and there I pretend to continue for some time...

6. **D.A.R.G.**: Letting fall an intentional veil over musical works, from not allowing wide physical or electronic division, to purposely releasing in favour of certain groups or individuals based on personal experience with them has been part of the modus operandi that characterizes you. What are the motives behind it? How could it be possible for those foreigners who are capable of appreciation and respect for dark sonic art to obtain physical copies of recordings of your different projects?

Ebvleb: In these times it is difficult for me to see all this so-called elitists, I do not see many of the so-called 'illuminated', and interesting Black Metal in terms of MUSIC and IDEOLOGY is difficult to find. While I have not started vinyl productions, it will be difficult for the world to find our TEMPLE OF PERVERSION; only producing vinyl can we make this stable, since only in this way will shipping costs be justified.

I despise the great majority of labels that dedicate themselves to edit garbage; I have created pseudo enemies for myself among individuals who are not worthy. Those who I could respect cannot comprehend, and those with who I am in contact and who are REAL, are very few. So I am not motivated to fight with the economy to disperse music in the world; however, I always hope that some label will once in a while approach with adequate intentions to our way of looking at production and distribution of our art.

I can only recommend that when you see our first 7" production then you should contact us and from there we will start our new era of productivity; we have unedited and upcoming recordings, besides pacts with bands that subscribe to our way of looking at the underground.

Evidently, we will also be within the reach of the populace and its vulgar appetite for rare vinyl, but this is part of what cannot be avoided if out in distribution.

You can only be underground if you really hate communication with inferior beings, mentally and spiritually speaking.

The few exceptions, like you, will be able to give faith that I am not easily accessible to the world and that I do not like to complicate myself with distribution; I am obsessed with being able to retake my paths and create the temple that BLACK METAL needs in the present to start a regeneration of BLACK SPIRITUALITY.

Before this happens, I am not available to the world and those who inhabit it.

7. **D.A.R.G.:** What is behind the connection between

ambient and black metal, which in your work appear to fuse

naturally, erasing borders in such a way that the illusion of differentiation becomes evident?

Ebvleb: This, I suppose, is emotional and sensory; Black Metal made with integrity manages a sinister structure that awakens black emotions, which are energies which can also be made to surface by Ambient made for spiritually dark beings; Black Emotionality.

It must be clarified that we are talking about Obscurantist music and separating whatever clone or imitation since if it is pure, the Art will be unique and unparalleled, just like each Master Mind is So.

8. **D.A.R.G.**: Some artists appear to find in pure improvisation the seeds which later dictate content, while others have a vision and dark energy that surrounds them in a way that leads them to seek a sound. I have the impression that the latter occurs in your case. In general, how relevant is this order of causes?

Ebvleb: None of them is, in themselves, relevant. What happens in this case is not improvising or composing, this is the expression of a moment that is lived and that is translated in sensation and emotion to a cumulus of humans, which can be either in a live setting or in private; each composition must be understood as a Being or an Entity that emanates and that expresses when it is interpreted.

During rehearsals one seeks, eternally, arrangements to the music and one finds more than are needed; the same must be selected and not all of them can remain in the final recording of a piece; however, those of us who experiment during concerts can maintain those arrangements which we liberate for our own satisfaction while at the same time transmitting new sonic figures.

Personally, I detest and abhor interpreting a piece in the exact same way two consecutive times; whichever the project that I am managing, my boredom is evident and I reject the absence of permanent interest in finding new forms and ways: nothing with life and energy of movement would remain always within a same sonic choreography, so to speak.

At the end of the path, I decide the forms and ways of my work in private; everything arises from my personal contact with the cosmos and its black energy that enters into contact with my thought at the moment of combining the same intentions and interests.

Another way, less mystic and ideological, would be for you to build a musical skeleton and then to play with its bones; besides that, you have spare bones for it, for any situation in which they are needed since they are all different and the fit each other perfectly (the segments).

What is transmitted through music must be absolutely, and in its totality, a SINCERE projection, and one that is very demanding with the individual, their possibilities and qualities of expression; if they are able is able to take comprehension of Darkness to a superior level, they may find a gap through which its chants and desires are expressed.

9. D.A.R.G.: In concerning the themes and methods of Abyssum and Nigromante, are these musical projects a spiritual medium acting as channeling?

Ebvleb: Presently, insofar as I handle the threads of composition in a total manner, I can say, write and clarify the following:

This is a conversation with dark energies through the music; in the case of ABYSSUM, my discussion is with the Cosmos, labyrinth of mysteries which only some of us can touch and thanks to this I am heard and it answers in various ways to my curiosity, for I have been able understand through my personal madness. This language could be taken by some idiot like telepathic but it is not so, these are energies to which we provide movement; with these I establish the conversation and it answers me through natural understanding, from which emanate the chemical reactions that they are able to transmit through my body, and in a very few times through 'the natural'... as you see, it is difficult for me to try and explain this through specific words for a publication, so he who understands should consider himself privileged for his understanding is superior to that of common humonkeys.

What must remain clear is that ABYSSUM is not "Thy Call"; that album was inspired by forests, storms, our nocturnal incursions into the mountains of our country; and we will clarify that "Poizon of god" is a darker album in regards to the absolute concept, the forests are far away from this atmosphere that relates more to closed and lugubrious environments, where solitude and candlelight accompany us more often than not; "Cvm foeda sanie ex ore" attempts to show Black Metal as a channel which, besides black emotion, can also transmit artistic superiority, and distances itself from that which are the ordinary bands, because orchestration is sought and Black Metal is thought of as an element that can be combined perfectly with Orchestrated music, and so this album is composed for it to be shown in some theatre with violins and other stringed instruments.

ABYSSUM handles diverse energies in composition, which, along with the basic and elemental matrix, is all that represents the dark and not sweet side of nature, and not absolute nature.

NIGROMANTE is a conversation with energies that have remained after having been created in humans; I consider that it is possible that we can leave behind energies that are captured, energies which are imperceptible when we attempt to locate them in specific places, but where they lie their bodies remain dispersed for whom makes themselves Medium; they must not be thought of strictly as energies as they are known.

Upon sensing these energies, I condition them to transmit emotions, messages which must be expressed so that those who are lost in death may go on along their way, if it exists, when liberating someone in some way in life, or they simply allow their energy to be diluted across the cosmos once more through asserting themselves by communicating me their laments in sonorous ways.

I repeat: we are cosmic dust and energy that mutes and transmutes. I consider that we are a cumulus of information which after having lived, returns, leaving behind data in the universe to it may nourish itself with knowledge that it cannot obtain by itself after having possessed a different form of life, but it may create forms, in this case like those of humans, which in their turn will create others from which the Cosmos will learn through their creation; so, using ordinary words: "receiving antennas" of information, we become non palpable veins.

10. **D.A.R.G.**: You have previously mentioned that intelligence and theology are incompatible. Are you referring to Christian Theology or is it applicable to all kinds of dogma, be it the crude idolatry of aboriginal Guatemalans or the new fashion in nordic countries and among black metal fans to seek refuge in a "spiritual" satanism?

Ebvleb: Theology, in general, is like believing in The Lord of the Rings, in superhumans, communication from gods to humans, but with a stupid and impulsive behaviour to justify itself; all that which misleads, and makes human beings avoid themselves is solely a matter of weakness.

A superior human being does not conform; he will believe in nothing else but himself and that which manifests in his life in an evident manner; he will find himself and will know what and how, during his existence, to allow his spirit to be contented to LIVE, which is a term that must be taken more deeply than that husk of the normal human being of wanting to be happy, and which is only a way of giving in to banality and all that which makes us retrogrades.

I am not someone who focuses on belonging to any specific zone on the planet, however, I am fortunate for the variety and comfort of nature in my country; but what the common Guatemalan is, I define as INFERIOR; all those who seek refuge and belongs to everything that surrounds them or a part of it, are in conclusion fearful of being alone with themselves, and this will remove him from true spirituality. My own personal way of living is one of dark tones; my taste is personal and not necessarily correct or incorrect, it simply is. I please my Spirit first; I use my body for that.

One does not need to look far to find an explanation for human weakness, they are simply not so intelligent or capable as they believe they are, neither those up nor those down. They are the same no matter how you look at them; very few superior human beings exist in the present, they are far too scarce to be distinctly noticeable, but little by little a thought is dispersed which will take many to understanding, and they will act more logically and less stupidly.

All that which leads humans to be conformist is a sickness; all that which looks beyond what is had and touched will be a mind that dedicates itself to be one with the cosmos, it will be the force that drives one to control the current and not allow one to be carried by it. It will be understood as an important part of the universe since we are living the flowering of that which human beings can become as a species if it survives its capacity of creation in addition to inferior behaviour.

Personally, [I believe that] nothing is correct or incorrect, it applies depending on the circumstances, but humans are banal par excellence and they hide themselves from logic, acting in coarse ways against all that which could make them take everything over more serious paths.

11. **D.A.R.G.**: Your observations regarding the mirage which is the idea of the glory of the old times echoes observations made by Varg Vikernes of Burzum with respect to the same. This person has also being marginalized by the same community that calls itself perverse and dark, judging him by an act of violence. Is it necessary for a scene to exist in order for transcendental art to be born? Is there any relation between an independent mind that looks for something precise yet wordless, and the concretization of that in great art? Is there a dichotomy between those who fight to maintain appearances and those who act to bring things into being?

Ebvleb: The desire of wanting to belong to something is already mediocre; transcendental Art sprouts from pure thoughts; the new has nowhere to fit since it is creating the cast; wasting time in [discussing] if the music had a moment of glory or a fall is to generalize; a solitary being who creates for himself cannot be made to fit among those who are appearances and who pretend to belong to something, to a herd; they do not strive to be the leader of that herd but to belong to it, and in my thinking, to be a leader in that herd is already unnecessary if one speaks of that which is Dark Spirituality; solitude is the basic and necessary magic.

The existence of a scene serves to generate an exchange of ideas; they allow thoughts to flow and intermingle; now, the term is so general that it admits the mixing of imitators, and human beings are by nature imitators, basic human behaviours are like this. An artist who places all kinds of impediments to growth before themselves is no artist, so it is no Superior Art which will sprout from Him, it will simply be art for humans, and those who value you are only inferior without [you] being able to gratify those of superior understanding; since there is Black Art in this planet which Honours with Integrity the exercise of this musical genre.

I will not deny that being able to meet human beings with whom it is a pleasure to exchange thoughts is enabled by the so-called scene; this fluidity of ideas among connoisseurs of similar tastes nourishes thought and catapults those who search to continue the search more intensely. In my case, I continue in solitude because I see that many paths are being taken and I seek my own, similar in some details to some currents but definitely taken to the inside, to the Abyss.

Disclaimer: This character you mention, I associate him with the fairy tale for children and nerds whose name I do not remember now but which he even relates in the cover art of his work. So I will not go into the details of such stupidity; what could such a man think, a human being who submerges himself in fairy tales and takes them to music, seems to me to lack depth; an absolute lack of black spirituality and is, instead only music, burning churches, orcs, "impulsive murder", "watch my video on youtube" ... fuck, "fuckin impostor."

It was due to that kind of human being that I decided to leave the term BLACK METAL since I was not able to endure feeling in some way that I belonged to that world ofclowns; ABYSSVM fathoms in a musical experiment of a very spiritual kind focused on the solitary and dark side on the human side, called "NEKROSPIRITUAL RAW METAL" and if I shall belong to something i will be along a very few brothers with whom we share similar tastes in music; the quality of music has very little to do with THE BLACK SPIRITUALITY OF THE ARTIST WHO CREATES MUSIC; and it is alright for there to be black metal for teenage rebels, but when that time passes or when you are simply intelligent, you desire to deepen and enter denser paths, beyond considerations of whether or not it is art or not, the manifestation emanates from human beings, it must reflect what the human being who expresses it is in themselves.

12. **D.A.R.G.**: Before, you have spoken about returning to a path or a way of thinking that existed in the past, which I interpret as an attitude of mystic discovery. Are you referring to your own methodologies, or to those of the genre or to a dark tradition, older and which goes beyond art in itself?

Ebvleb: If we speak about creating a temple for dark music, I am referring to that in itself, without pretending who is more or less; but it is obvious that I consider that there are certain characters in this planet who deserve to be taken in by something that dignifies them beyond and which rewards them in banality, and what better than a Thinking circle. Besides, it should not be kept secret that personally, being able to help artists worthy of the genre grow would be something that would reward me personally; musically there are great beings creating incredible art and grounding their own beliefs, aside from my sharing them or not, they dignify themselves on their own, even with their mistakes or successes.

If it is a questioning that seeks a tradition, it is INCORRECT; I do not share the idea of looking into something that is already done, this is like taking what was left behind and picking it up; that which is mystical in a natural way in its behaviour does not belong to a before or an after, it does not enter dreams and it only sees the present reality with a different lenses. In past times, man looked more toward the inner since he did not have so many mirrors upon which to look at himself physically; all this has malnourished man's behaviour, and so he who does not yet know himself is always considering that in some past there existed an answer that is no more, which is ridiculous and stupid. To seek in the distant past which is not known by a personal experience the answer to something: it is mediocre.

13. **D.A.R.G.**: How does your art differ from what many nowpopular bands do with symbols, terminology, customs and religious postures?

Ebvleb: I do not seek to express anything through symbols or religious systems. The collective can go fuck itself (I say it again); it is for that same reason that I do not listen to that kind of music; the big bands, excepting Inquisition, I do not respect. It is not that I share their [Inquisition's] way of thinking, but their behaviour is that of authentic Dark gentlemen and that should be respected even though our way of thinking differs.

Whosoever wastes their time in so much paraphernalia does not search too deeply, and is only into music for music in itself; this will be confusing for those who are merely normal.

14. **D.A.R.G.**: Could you summarize the black spirituality and temple and what they could give to black metal as a source with foundations beyond the mundane and pretentious?

Ebvleb: I do not seek to give black metal anything; I have distanced ABYSSVM from that term, now we are beyond, not necessarily better or worse; we are simply in a musical path which we travel in solitude. From the beginnings of this musical experiment we have expressed that ABYSSVM needs to be felt more than understood; if you allow yourselves to flow with the whole of the musical ideas and you are able to perceive the Dark Energy, we will all be satisfied; contrariwise, you will not be attracted to what we do and what we try to transmit.

15. **D.A.R.G.**: Is the obscurantism inherent in the musical essence of Abyssum construed on purpose? Are the subtleties hidden deliberately or are they simply hidden by virtue of finding themselves buried under layers of elaborations that occur naturally during the composition of eloquent and

perfectionist music?

Ebvleb: I do not consider that ABYSSVM should be seen as a musical band; it is itself a matrix that creates beings who come alive and who make themselves. I cannot explain how a theme creates itself, not accepting the fusion in a sincere and honest way without compassion or pity, the only thing I need to do is to find that matrix riff whence everything shall arise; in making itself, it will know where to accrue itself.

Obviously, I consider myself to be an exceedingly intelligent person, which gives me a deeper spirituality, and which spirituality seasons my honest behaviour since I am not afraid to face that which surrounds me. To apply this to music is to enter in passion, which in this case causes in me dark music; and it is dark because that is how it feels, there is no better term to describe it, or at least man has not invented one yet. For many it is wickedness, aggression, perversion, etc., human behaviours, all too human.

I must repeat that this thing called composition is a conversation between the cosmos and the understanding which it gave me; the conversation is the expression of my way of feeling it, and I understand rendering gratitude to it for having been given the opportunity to be in life what I am. The Infernal Guide, in my own terms, not what human beings necessarily understand as infernal... I am the Voice of the Cosmos; Wrath from a beyond.

16. **D.A.R.G.**: We could say that art possesses an essence and an aesthetic; aesthetic being the form in which essence is encapsulated and transmitted, and which essence is then recreated within the human being that receives the form. Could any aesthetic be used to transmit any essence, or are aesthetics (form, structure), seen esoterically, an inseparable part and medium of all that is music and, therefore, essence and aesthetics are inseparable?

Ebvleb: I do not believe in rules, compositional norms in any sense; each Artist has the option of choosing the path and manner of his ART; making it clear that I am speaking about artists, [in regards to] some vagabond rocknroller I am not sure they can transmit more than that which can be observed in themselves, nor is it important for me to judge the behaviour of others to distance myself from the discomfort that they may cause for me. The chants of ABYSSVM are beings with a different life, they have nothing to do with "aesthetics" or esoteric tendencies. This which we create is essence of our belief, and how it is seen, expressed, listened, is nothing more than expression of that which is created in the moment, which in my case is an entering into conversation with the Universe, [myself] being scientist devoted to exploration through the inhabiting for a time this species called "human"; I search and will search for that which produces Obscurantist curiosity.

17. **D.A.R.G.**: If we completely removed lyrics, names, imagery and any other extra-musical reference, should the essence and musical character be perceivable, or does this latter depend on the aforementioned elements?

Ebvleb: Music is to be felt, a medium of expression to transcend life; if Music is created as ART, it will by itself express what will be inevitably felt as its essence; the character will logically be perceived if one is not the creator, as a result of the spiritual essence of who "listens", [but] this is already a posteriori to the important thing which is the moment of creation.

18. **D.A.R.G.**: Can black metal become, as obscurantist music, in an esoteric tool, the study of and meditation upon which without need for words, symbols or abstractions, may promote in one a conscious development of human potential?

Ebvleb: IT DEPENDS ON EACH INDIVIDUAL; I CAN ONLY SPEAK FOR MYSELF. Through music and in all that is "CREATION" emanating from me, I do not see symbols that are even similar [elsewhere]; I simply express myself for an entity called UNIVERSE / COSMOS; nothing that is human can help me with this, beyond that which sprouts from my being as a living creature that breathes and thinks.

19. **D.A.R.G.**: Does music reveal aspects outside the artist's control, perhaps even unconscious aspects, in a way that music itself expresses truth more than the words, explanations and lyrics by said artist?

Ebvleb: A weak artist can only create weak music, but only those who are superior to that weakling will see the truth for themselves, and those who are equal to that weak being will believe it as the truth; everything must be taken in accordance to its source. In my case I am rarely fooled by false expressions; in many cases they reveal themselves on their own account. In others cases, one must pay attention, but I well know what kind of humans they are just by listening to their music; before me many things are revealed which evidence them.

20. **D.A.R.G.**: Given that reality is what it is, independently of the screens and illusions that humans place before it, is it more probable that a logical order and organization of the universe exists, even if we have not deciphered it completely yet? Or is it all, as some religious devotional currents (self-denominated black or white) say, all chaos and irrationality beyond human comprehension? Is our present condition an intermediate state that is discovering and partially capturing the cosmic system?

Ebvleb: I like to think that we are an extension of the universe itself, its creation but at the same time that we are Him/That; we are a simple process; in my case I do not doubt the existence at a distance of forms of intelligent life, even superior to humans; I believe that each cosmic system captures through us, we are united for the better or the worse, the process of.

We are simply a species on this planet who dominates by force; according to how we will develop ourselves as a species, we will be given the rewards of slowly opening up the unending mysteries of life and the universe. Personally, I apply myself to being grateful for inhabiting on this occasion such a strange species in its development, an arrogant species that feels superior and is simply a part OF; but I am allowed to feel this way and I take advantage of my moment in life to enter the chasms of the Spirit, whose existence is an absolute mystery.

Now, when you say OUR, I step aside since I an obviously not the same as the vast majority of humans; I distance myself from a simple simian evolved and I intend to be a DEEP SOUL.

21. **D.A.R.G.**: What does the aforementioned nature of the cosmos imply about the music that lies within it, and which consequently follows its rules just as our minds and bodies?

Ebvleb: I do not know if music lies within Cosmos, or if the music sprouts from it creation to self-marvel of what it cannot create and study on its own but through what humans call Nature; it is obvious that music is not exclusive to humans. Furthermore, for me music has no rules, rules were set by humans to be able, so to speak, to give shape to music and reinterpret it in diverse ways.

ESOTERIC NIHILISM

A discovery of reality beyond utter destruction

I

Brett Stevens' Nihilism is a compilation of thoughts collected through years of philosophical exploration, and it condenses a clarified version of what he terms nihilism, though this is not necessarily the simplified idea that the masses of pseudo educated simians would understand. Instead of being simply defined by a lack of belief in values, it offers the only sensible metaphysical exposition which could make a case for it; this is a lack of belief in inherent value, and through it a destruction of everything that is merely a human construct. The work is not so much a logical argument for the stance, but an exposition of the benefits of adopting it. In other words, it is an advocacy of nihilism, and not the opening of a dialogue or debate regarding its worth. In this, Brett Stevens parts from the assumption that communication (in the sense of imparting real knowledge rather than merely information) between human beings is impossible through direct means such as speaking or writing. Instead, it is expected that those who possess a seed of the talent or character that is required to arrive to certain realizations will do so in time through introspection and experience.

The question of necessity for nihilism such as is espoused by Brett Stevens is answered by Friedrich Nietzsche himself in the preface to the Will to Power, where he states that the old values have run their course by coming to their ultimate conclusions. In other words, Nihilism is used as a way to clean the slate and find new values. Like Friedrich Nietzsche, Brett Stevens does not consider that Nihilism should be an end in itself, but a tool that will allow us to be a constant state of alert, that values are discovered in a realist way; this way means evaluating how a certain idea responds to specific circumstances, rather than applying them as a matter of fact without any discernment as to whether they are suitable. One could also describe nihilism as being sceptical of everything yet at once being open to revelations of all kinds: Nothingness as a portal to Being.

The way in which Esoteric Nihilism differs from empiricism is that rather than being a reduction of truth to sensory experience, it consists in the elimination of all except that which is necessary and evident. Necessity and self-evidence, furthermore, are determined by external and internal states alike, applying them realistically, and then transcendentally as well. For the esoteric nihilist, there is no absolute or relative truth, and the adjectives 'subjective' and 'objective' cease to have any relevant meaning. In essence, nihilism is an extreme realist position that adheres to input from reality; it also differs from a mere empiricism in that nihilism would even reject the materialist posture that does away with the value of inner experience as a way to truth.

To discover the grain of this Esoteric Nihilism is to realize that all philosophy, ideology and ideas in general are constructs, abstractions, even those that tend to emphasize the grosser aspects of reality to the obfuscation of the subtler psychological and transcendent ones. Some have argued (in what is but an absurdist but quite popular logically fallacious argumentation) that the preceding definition must include the philosophy that makes the statement itself, hence invalidating itself in the process. The Esoteric Nihilist classification of said ideations, however, does not discount their contingent usefulness, but that, in a last analysis, they do not constitute reality itself.

II

IN A BOOK OF THREE Inspirations, Tsong Khapa the Great explains a current of Tibetan cosmogonic philosophy which adopts the name of The Middle View. He says that such sects adopting this description avoid the extremes of what he calls reification and nihilism. This is achieved by keeping in mind, on the one hand, that everything is transitory, impermanent, and thus not real; on the other hand, it is observed that the universe works through consistent and infallible laws. To better explain what the esoteric philosophy of Nihilism actually consists of, the book is divided into three main parts; namely, Nihilism, Realism and Trascendentalism. From a functional point of view, these symbolize the three elements that should take an adept application of the ideas exposed. However, rather than seeing them as a series of steps to take, they are tools to utilize, precepts to apply with care, finding a balance that allows us to detach ourselves from abstraction while remaining not anchored, but in dynamic contact with our raw perceptions of reality.

Like so, in his book, Ride the Tiger, Julius Evola considers Nietzsche the perfect nihilist precisely because the philosopher had lived nihilism and had overcome it. He goes on to observe that Nietzsche, in fact, considered nihilism as a transitional stage, and corresponding to a pathological mind. Even more importantly, Evola reminds us that Nietzsche already hailed the countermovement which should come to displace nihilism. Brett Stevens names this going beyond, Transcendentalism, which is not an obliteration of Nihilism, but rather an edifice built after the necessary purging which the latter makes possible.

The destruction of abstractions through the upholding of pure Nihilism can be described in the words Heidegger uses in his Introduction to Metaphysics, where he describes nihilism as a reduction of the universe to current beings, and thence to a treatment of Being itself as nothing. Heidegger also describes pure nihilism as the disregard for the fundamental law of thinking, thence destroying faith and undermining the possibility of constructs. This is the cleansing which Evola argues Nietzsche speaks of, and which cleansing stage is to be transcended. From the point of view of Esoteric Nihilism, insofar as the Heideggerean (cosmic) Being is unknowable, it is irrelevant, yet its existence and presumed originating or emanating role is not necessarily denied, simply set aside.

Such is the void which Brett Stevens summons forth here, a universe of possibilities strictly according to what is and can be as per an infinite yet grounded discovery at every level of consideration, whether it be physical, mental or spiritual, as all are interconnected in many ways. The way opened up by such an outlook is one dignified by self-reliance, and invested in the principle of responsibility, in the sense that each action is recognized as having consequences, whatever these might be. In the latter thought, there is no presumption of the moral kind, but rather, a stoic acceptance of the current of experiences and choices that constitute life.

III

MORE AKIN TO ESOTERIC methodologies and covert mysticism than Nietzsche, Brett Stevens embraces Nihilism as a mantra in constant declamation, a magical spell over which one is to constantly rise above in a trance-like mental action. A mirage appears, and some confuse the actions here described with empiricism, missing the Transcendentalism that Bret Stevens raises above Nihilism as if in separate, parallel universes in collision. What we see is closer to art than to philosophy, in truth, because the highest human faculties are reached through the totality of a Royal Art, and not through the purely rationalist mind.

And while shying away from outright religiosity, it appears relevant here to mention the spiritualized nihilism of which Nikolas Schreck speaks in Demons of the Flesh, a popular book on Tantric Left Hand Path practices. What interests us here is Schreck's description of this Path's goal, which might not be wholly inapplicable to Brett Stevens' Nihilism. Schreck says this is not the dissolution of the self into the greater whole (which is the goal of Right Hand doctrines of 'illumination') but rather a strengthening of the practitioner's psyche by way of an attack on illusions on the one hand, and a constant discovery of crude reality on the other. Individuality, rather than individualism, as Brett Stevens would express it, in the championing of the unique striving of each individual for truth through experience and inner realization. This leads to a supreme exaltation that distinguishes the excellent individual from the complacent, mediocre minds that substitute truth and holistic realization with vapid entertainment and empty accomplishment.

Lawrence Birken, in his Hitler as Philosophe, describes National Socialism as embodying an apparent mixture of Traditionalism and Modernity, which does away with the superstitious exotericism of religions once and for all, while maintaining ideals of perfection to strive for endlessly towards recurring improvement in harmony with nature. Esoteric Nihilism, now explained as Traditionalist, could be compared to a National Socialism minus modernism; that is, without its Marxist-influenced elements, replacing them instead with a Traditional Western Pagan outlook. Where Hitler called for an adoption of modern methods that could respond to modern conditions with efficiency, Brett Stevens sees in this an error, a compromise of sorts that can only lead to disaster as the source of all problems is the spirit of modernity itself. In short, what must be fought are not the temporary conditions, which are the outer, the symptoms, of decadence.

It should be added to our discussion, that Brett Stevens' method is not post-modern, since at some point the thinker advocates a strict Traditionalism. This Traditionalism, moreover, is composed of an intelligent application of rules to the unique conditions of any point in time. Here is a dynamism that preserves timeless truths throughout a constantly changing set of states. As such, the ideas that Brett Stevens wishes to shine forth by the advocacy of Nihilism are but a finer, pleasant and sober exposition of truths recurrent since time immemorial. Traditionalism seen from within, moreover, is understood as the living of human life in accordance to immanent truths which make up reality, constants in the pattern language of reality.

An Interview with Brett Stevens

1. D.A.R.G.: Regarding ancient Indian schools of thought, Agehananda Bharati writes that these are not so much branches of philosophy, in the sense that we understand classical Greek philosophy, but rather ideology. Would you describe the esoteric nihilism you propose as philosophical or ideological? Is it both?

Brett Stevens: If we were to differentiate between ideology and philosophy, it would make sense to say that ideology consists of prescriptive ideas or moral "oughts," things that we "should" do, where philosophy describes the world and offers us as a series of cause-effect postulates of the nature, "If you do X, you will receive results Y, Z and secondary consequences W, V." In this sense he seems correct to me in that schools of thought build upon a base philosophy and say that if this philosophy is understood as realistically accurate, it then implies the following interpretation which leads to prescriptive deductions. In this way, he is separating the schools of thought from the original philosophy. It seems to me that he may be only partially correct because the prescriptive reading requires an interpretation of the philosophy, which as Fred Nietzsche reminds us, is a philosophy in itself much like our mental objects are copies of things found in reality.

The esoteric nihilism that I propose takes the form of philosophy because at its core it is not prescriptive at all, and its philosophical approach is as a framework which, while being a case of the rare complete philosophy in itself, functions as a gateway to other philosophies and a means of interpreting the broader field of all philosophy. It is thus a replacement for ideology, which normally is used as a filter and interpretive guide for philosophy because ideology is closer to real-world questions – such as "What is the best life?" and "How should we live?" – and for that reason people necessarily encounter it before philosophy, but in itself, is the opposite of an "ought" question; it is descriptive, not prescriptive. On top of that, however, certain observations become unavoidable, leading to nihilist interpretations of longstanding historical tendencies in humanity.

Its esoteric nature prohibits it from being an ideology as we know them in the modern sense, which is where our definitions may deviate from those of Agehananda Bharati. After equality is established as a goal as happened in the West with The Renaissance,™ all ideas become ideas for manipulating masses of people toward the evident conclusions that follow the assumptions coded into those ideas, and then those people move as a mass toward those conclusions. Esoteric ideas more resemble a series of staircases and doorways, with the mass starting at the bottom and reaching only through the first couple levels, after which point only select others go on, building on each portion or broadening detail of the idea as they go, then having risen above to the point where they see their previous idea in a new context – similar to the modern idea of "retroactive continuity" – they find a new doorway at the top of the stairs from whence they are looking down on the previous opened door. This is the process of philosophy, more than ideology.

Ideology suffers from a fatal flaw in that it counteracts natural selection. When you set out the rules for success, people can follow them without understanding them, and without the inner desire to do good that is required to understand the reasons for them. They are merely conforming to succeed. In this sense, formal and written doctrines are inferior to informal and esoteric ones, which usually begin with a few common sense ideas and expand outward, requiring the esoteric progression of staircases and doorways described above. By doing this, these philosophies "fail gracefully" meaning that they collapse at the local level, rather than perpetuating bad data wherever they exist. Paganism failed this way by, when Western civilization grew too large and successful and the rise in lower caste people meant that keeping the herd together took up too much energy for people to focus on the purpose and goals of Western civilization, simply dying out in each village but never being co-opted and corrupted as later happened to Christianity, a simplified version of Paganism codified with ideological imperatives within it. Later attempts to resurrect paganism have been almost all comedic and have not been seen as credible for this reason.

Nihilism offers a view that has been informed by The Human Problem, or why all of our organizations and groups eventually fail. Essentially, as any group succeeds, focus changes from its purpose to its maintenance so that individuals can appreciate its benefits, and these individuals create as many internal goals are there are people. A healthy organization has many paths leading to the same goal; a sick one has many paths leading to different goals. This victory for entropy – "thermodynamics has won at a crawl," per W.S.B. – afflicts every union of two or more people over time, and is a result of a swelling of members of the group who do not or cannot understand its purpose and goals. It occurs through success, in that anything which is popular attracts more people or allows more people to survive, at which point the lack of natural selection joins the unbalanced ratio of those who understand its purpose to those who do not and those doom the organization.

2. **D.A.R.G.**: Heidegger reads in some fragments by Parmenides the exposition of a threefold path, which he explains is unitary. This path, he says, consists in the first place in the way to Being, which is unavoidable; secondly, in the way to Nothing, which is inaccessible; and thirdly, in the way to seeming, which is always accessible and travelled. How does Nihilism figure into this metaphysical portrait, if at all?

Brett Stevens: Nihilism possesses a similar but less formalized recognition of three layers which exist simultaneously in life. They are:

i. The world of the senses: this has two components that it is material and physical, and that it is in the present tense. When we turn to our sensations, we become aware of this world, often yanking us back out of wool gathering or other mental experience. Most importantly, this world is tangible and thus seems irrefutable, because in the moment we can touch, feel, smell, taste, and otherwise engage in what feels like direct experience of the material world. The deception here is that even in the present tense, we are in the past, because it takes our brains some microseconds to process input, tokenize it, characterize it, relate it to objects in memory, and then present it to our decisionmaking conscious minds through a complex series of balances which assess relevance and likelihood of accuracy.

ii. The invisible world: in this world, we are looking at knowledge of logic as a means of predicting the world. This process reveals a fundamental trauma that all humans endure, which is the possibility of being wrong in our estimate about the world, whether throwing a ball and having it end up elsewhere than where we intended it to be, or making complex financial calculations that turn out to be incorrect. In either case, we risk losing rank in the social hierarchy of our peers by being revealed as less competent than others. The invisible world requires us to make logical predictions based on knowledge of how the world has operated in the past, extrapolated from disparate events, and to then apply it to the situation before us, and failure to do this shows a lesser degree of fundamental connection to reality and ability within it. Since this world exists between the present and future consequences, it implicates both long-term thinking and the ability to understand the logical principles and patterns of the world around us, especially those that are invisible because like gravity or standard distributes, they are part of the inner structure of the universe.

iii. Underlying reality: this can never be experienced because it is not a physical thing, but an emergent property of the interaction of different forces and objects, and in this interaction as participants, we influence the outcome. Like Schroedinger's cat, reality is not what it is until it is experienced, and even then, there is a high degree of variability, as if we move through many different iterations of this reality based on our decisions. Cause-effect reasoning comes into play here, because what we perceive is the effect, or rather an image of the effect rendered by our minds, and the causes can never be directly known to us, so we must intuit them based on our inner knowledge of how our own existence and that of reality around us share many parallels.

Contrary to what most people believe, nihilism focuses on the second and not the first. Its concern is with removing the human elements of wishful thinking, projection, tunnel vision, misunderstandings of causality, and rationalization that distort our ability to understand the world. As a result, it immediately boils down reality to its logical elements, and from those, uses pattern comparison to extrapolate what other parts of reality are like, since reality is fundamentally consistent and repeats patterns in parallel across different media – thought, information, matter, energy – because these patterns, like Plato's forms, are innate to its core process of creating and maintaining itself. Our goal is to understand those root patterns by analysis and intuition, much like someone using sonar to scope out the sea floor and understand what might be down there.

3. **D.A.R.G.:** In relation to the aesthetics of art, can

Nihilism help us extrapolate from reality at large in order to narrow down a methodology for assimilating, channelling and organizing (in other words, composing) works of art?

Brett Stevens: A friend of mine once opined that art was not the artobject, but two stages of a process: the artist conceptualizing the experience that was to be communicated, and the observer using their own creative imagination to understand what the artist was communicating by noticing where it was "profound," or expressed something of the core attributes of the human experience of life. Nihilism helps art by redirecting us from sensual experience, social experience, and solipsistic mental experience toward a perception of reality, and then by denying that communication exists, allowing us to instead make gestures that require the audience to meet us halfway and by going through the interpretive process, undertake the same artistic journey made by the artist and through that, intuit the same knowledge of reality, life and humanity that the artist encoded in the work. This could be expressed like the computer science notion of "Model, View, and Controller"; the art is the data, artistry the controller, and both artist and observer are experiencing views of that underlying model, just like we do with life itself, deriving suppositions about a world we can never directly experience, and then comparing them to other knowledge to knock out inconsistencies and discover the pattern language of reality.

4. **D.A.R.G.**: Correctly understood, one could say that Nihilism escapes the trap of utilitarianism and individualism only by virtue of the fact that only minds capable of grasping

the need and way to parallelism and transcendence can make use of it in the first place. Could you walk us through the long, and wide, range of vision that the devastation and free fall of Nihilism makes necessary in order to survive it and properly make use of it?

Brett Stevens: Nihilism fits the profile of a fall from grace. That is, we start out in life believing in a warm and nurturing universe, and after being introduced to the human world, become cynical and somewhat hopeless when we see how most people think, what motivates them, and the endless corruption of their behavior in groups. In order to accept nihilism, one must come to desperation with this world, much as one must to undertake any serious religious, occult or transformative philosophical experience. The narrative that people advance through social behavior – that humanity is a better order than nature, and that for us all to get along, we must accept everyone regardless of their relevance to purpose or internal degree of force of intellect and force of character – must reveal itself to be fundamentally toxic, not just wrong but a direction away from all that is good in life.

At that point, great despair and aimlessness settles over most people. Few go any further, and instead attempt to distract themselves with the physical and sensual, as the 1960s hippies did. But for those who push further, a great calm awaits. This is the death of the neurosis that compels most people to move frenetically through life and to obsessively pay attention to the social environment around them. The budding nihilist lets this fall away, and instead begins his or her study of the parts of reality that are closest to personal experience. From there, patterns emerge, and these can then be applied elsewhere, which starts to open doors to similarities and through that, to a deeper look at the implication of those patterns and the type of language of patterns that they imply.

From there, the new nihilist can move on to more challenging things. Generally, this stage exhibits a hunger for "real" data as opposed to that which is socially-mediated, so there are many walks in ancient forests and reading of classical texts, but most importantly, as Bruce Charlton writes, a process of spending time alone and in silence thinking, as a means of discovering the linkages between intuition and reality and creativity, seizes the initiate. It is worth mentioning that we are speaking of the top eighth of the population by intelligence here as those eligible to make it to this stage. Beyond it awaits a challenge, and then gradual but not linear expansion of knowledge.

These challenges appears because of the collision between the newfound knowledge and not the world, but our own inclination to rationalize, deduce, filter out the unsafe, explain the world as good, and inflate our own ego. After the ego-death that comes after successfully defeating this challenge, the initiate undergoes the process of transcendence, by which the universe starts to make sense not just on a minimal functional level, but as an optimization for beauty and greatness, and at that point it becomes not just logical, but aesthetically and morally beautiful. This stage requires crossing a great void of fear, and afterwards, nothing can ever be the same.

5. **D.A.R.G.**: Is an esoteric nihilism better understood in the context of full Tantric practices and indications, beyond the cliché of sexual, amoral practices, that is. If not, what can it be allied or compared to?

Brett Stevens: Tantra presents one form of an eternal way of thinking which is inherent to esotericism, and which Varg Vikernes describes as "syncretic eclecticism." It means an interweaving of knowledge from different sources, comparing the patterns, and finding the principles and framework that is suggested by those, much as Plato describes the discovery of forms. At some point, the initiate is left with a profound sense that the universe is comprised of mathematical or informational principles, and that the physical is merely an effect of those, which opens the door not just to monistic metaphysics but also an understanding of relativity. Esotericism describes a process by which learning is cumulative and found in all areas of existence, meaning that there is no specific discipline, only a generalized use of the intellect, creativity and intuition to explore what is found in the world and derive its principles, then compare those in a matrix of cycles to what is known and what else is being known, allowing those patterns to emerge. This corresponds to the third and fourth paragraphs in the previous answer.

6. **D.A.R.G.**: As far as our conversation goes, Nihilism is a portal, but it is also a method, once it is understood after the first stage, in which we "fall" and see everything fall apart in front of our eyes. How can this method, which some would relate to and indeed reduce to skepticism and empiricism, indeed make room for mysticism? If it does, is pantheism the only logical result since, in your own words, "the underlying world can never be experienced"?

Brett Stevens: There is an awakening and "fall from grace" period in which one becomes aware of the human world which is composed of false universals based on lowest common denominator concepts of truth, values, and communication and how incorrect it is regarding both the natural, logical, and physical world and the metaphysical world implied by logic which exists enclosing that physical world. Nihilism launches us out of a world of universal absolutes which are actually human desires and wishful thinking, and instead makes us accept a focus on reality and therefore, a study of nuance as opposed to boxy, broad, and controlling categories and moral absolutes.

Once this fall from grace is accomplished, however, we have attained a gateway philosophy. We now know how to think about things as a starting point, and from that, there is some degree of implicit purpose depending on the initiate and the degree of his abilities and desire to push forward. For most, the initial realization of nihilism is enough; the human world is lies, so we pay attentions to the patterns of reality instead and see what we can notice, realizing that if another person is talking to us they are most likely lying and at best, are using symbols only they understand in the hope that we can approximate their tokens, meet them halfway, interpret their meaning, and, by going down a similar path ourselves, reach the same conclusion.

When you and I talk, I have a well-founded expectation that you are trying to communicate something that you have learned, are excited about it and attempting in the fullness of moral goodness to be accurate, and are hoping that I am also excited about it. I do not have the same expectation with others; I anticipate them to be using some game theory of their own, which is a tripartite: (1) trying to advance themselves to a top position while (2) attempting to conceal this fact behind illusions of being human, utilitarian, and pluralistic but (3) simultaneously trying to send the rest of us down the rabbit-hole of human wishful thinking. Every good con man knows that the game is to use the momentum of the mark — the target of the con — against him. You pitch him a vision, but you are careful like

a lawyer or politician to use words in their technical meanings, instead of how you know he will understand them. You tell him that a product will improve his sex appeal by 500%; he tries and cannot get laid in a whorehouse, so he comes back to you and you say, "We did improve your sex appeal from a tenth of a percent to fifty percent, but that's still too low to even seduce a herpetic goat, but we have another product that might help." The mark, greedy for power and wealth, conned himself and you just led him on. Nihilism involves recognizing that most human conversation, like 99% of it, is simply a con job and that the way to avoid being conned is to look at language as exactly what it is, shared tokens with boundaries known as categories, and to realize that people are cleverly playing with those categories (sex appeal by 500%) in order to sell their product, idea, or personal power while making us the victims of ourselves. If you ask me, this is why people fear nihilism: it means the gig is up for your average human, which is basically just a talking monkey with car keys trying to convince other monkeys to do something for it so that it can increase its standing in the troupe. For most people, this nihilist realization is the greatest utility they will find from the philosophy.

However, some will want to push onward. At this point, we have to ask whether there is a conflict between nihilism and beliefs, values, cultures, customs, gods, or a belief in an afterlife, and the answer is that of course there is not; nihilism simply commands that we realize that there is no universal truth, values, or communication.

What does that mean, in the context of metaphysics? First, that individual humans do not share the same understanding of the world, and the same applies to metaphysics; even more, since understanding creates attraction per the law of attraction and allows for realization in the world of quantum physics, to use a modern metaphor, we will not get the same results out of metaphysics. Someone who has focused mental state and clarity of intuition may encounter different levels of existence much as they are able to visualize different structures in the physical world. Others may look deep into their minds and find a lump of mud.

We have different destinies, all of us human individuals, just as plants and animals do under natural selection. Some go farther than others. This also applies to values and communication. What we understand as important and can apply with self-discipline constitutes our values. Some men are finer than others, as Jane Austen would say, on the level of behaviour, which reflects an underlying distinction of intellect and intuition; they see more, and respond to it, where the ordinary person is just another animal stumbling along looking to eat, fornicate, defecate, and agitate for more power without regard to whether he can use it well or even if he needs it.

Every prole wants to be a king; every king just wants a kingly decision made. A king can be a nihilist and have a profound understanding of metaphysics and spirituality, but for your average person, the situation has already become too complex to be anything but a muddle. What this means is that the primary conflict with nihilism and religion is between nihilism and the exoteric, egalitarian, and individualistic doctrines through which most people understand religion; a nihilist will take an entirely different approach and reach different places.

Ultimately, nihilism commands that we study reality including humanity instead of the other way around, and so we see the brutal truth of what humans are, but at the same time, are open to studying anything which is real. That gets complex when we talk about the esoteric, where different people not just receive different results but trigger different results.

What might a nihilist view of metaphysics look like? As Plato pointed out, our existence is the effect of more complex causes. In this way, multiple "worlds," dimensions, levels, and layers can exist within the same logical structure, with our physical world being one of them. It turns out that the Earth is not the center of our planet cluster and therefore we rotate around the sun and not vice-versa. The same is true of metaphysics: our physical world is not the ultimate condition, but one of many, and they are all united by the same logical rules and principles.

This viewpoint, called "monism," shows up everywhere from Johannes Eckart, Immanuel Kant, and Arthur Schopenhauer through the true ancients, the Hindu sages, Nordic poets, and the Greco-Romans who codified similar principles. Those views in turn are ten to twenty thousand years decayed from the original Indo-European religion which was probably as cryptic as the Nords and Greeks but more clarifying like the Hindus.

On the other side, however, humans have a tendency to corrupt anything they can with their desires for a human world; we call this tendency "crowdism" and when applied to religion, we get "dualism," or the notion that there is one set of rules and logical postulates for this world, and then another better world where all of those are turned upside down. In saner times we would call that ironism or contrarianism as a philosophy, but people love the idea of a perfect heaven of doing nothing which is their reward for being obedient to the morality of the herd, and a fiery hell full of sodomy for those who violate the rules of the herd.

This means that the nihilist navigates a difficult path between atheism, which relies on the material to predict the broader monist world, and dualism, which is an exoteric vision of the spiritual. As with all things, understanding nuance and structure instead of the categories which humans use to contain their fears is essential here.

7. **D.A.R.G.**: Veering into the practical would need this philosophical outlook, which of necessity is suspended above particulars enough to sustain validity throughout times, to have a distinct praxis. It is understood that what elitists would call worthy minds should be able to discern and derive such methodologies on their own to apply a philosophy pragmatically. However, would it be possible to create layers around Esoteric Nihilism so that it could be used as a practical guide over a more generalized demography? If so, what would this entail?

Brett Stevens: One of the most enduring ideas from Spengler was his observation that the ancient Greeks were healthiest when they built their monuments and temples of wood and not stone. Their understanding was that there is only one form of tradition, a living one, and that the more one makes it exoteric by writing it down and building permanent conditioners of it such as statues, the less alive it is and therefore it will not fail gracefully by fading away but will instead become a zombie version of itself, much like Catholicism and libertarianism did as described in the answer to the first question in this interview. The pagans wrote nothing down and formalized nothing, and so we have no record of them, but at the same time, we do not have a robotic undead Pagan church which has become a tool of the crowdists; Christians, conservatives, and libertarians cannot say the same. For this reason, I suggest a twofold approach: first, that our praxis be encoded in stories, where we can see the why behind certain general types of practices, and second, that it never be formally encoded as procedure, only symbol. This allows those who should be practicing to do it and excludes most of the others.

8. **D.A.R.G.**: What does Esoteric Nihilism tells us about what reality asks of our character as humans in order to not only survive but excel? What of our species, in order to evolve towards higher capacities, in every area or, more completely and as ancient Vedic philosophy would express it, "in the three worlds"?

Brett Stevens: We could see esoteric nihilism as the ancestor of Tradition and conservatism, meaning that it is both (a) focused on results in reality over human feelings, desires, and judgments and (b) has some transcendental aspect, meaning that if you seek to conserve the best of the past, you must know what "best" is and therefore need to know "excellence." These two things keep themselves in balance; instead of the prescriptive, we have a general outlook toward the qualitative, and a transcendental goal of excellence, goodness, truthfulness (realism), and beauty, and to balance the tendency to launch off in pursuit of unrealistic ideals, we partner it to hard realism. These two can only exist in parallel, which is part of their beauty. One without the other becomes self-neutralizing, much like nature makes homosexuals or ugly people out of bad genetic combinations, ensuring that those genes die with them.

This general approach leads toward certain realizations of a timeless way of life that maximizes humanity by, like an accelerated natural selection, pushing us toward greater excellence and therefore, producing more people of genius; as esotericists, we believe in the necessity of people of genius because only they can go further along the esoteric path in terms of ability, and we need a large number of them because only some of them will have the second component of esotericism, which is the will to learn in this area. Some geniuses will turn toward martial arts or the natural sciences, but among the rest will be found those inclined toward philosophy, literature, and leadership, all of which require some steps taken on the path. The "genius pump" made Western Civilization great, and probably existed in other times as well, but when those civilizations turned from it, they fell into decay.

A classical civilization begins with the idea of social order as a component of natural order. We see that predation and hierarchy exist in nature so instead of opting for a different quantity, meaning an alternative to those, we instead seek to position them in the right places within the natural order so that these inevitable things work for us instead of us against us. For example, when the strong and good subjugate and enslave the weak and bad, this is a victory; when the good do good to the good and bad to the bad, this is natural selection and morality in parallel union; when as a result, the best rise above the rest and more of the best are produced, this is evolution instead of "progress" toward a Utopia through equality. This is why classical civilization tends to be rigorously undemocratic, ignorant of humanism, and geared toward understanding the natural world and its metaphysical component.

Within that civilization, you tend to find an aristocratic leadership, a caste system based around the homes of the aristocrats as employers of the lower castes, a strong culture and religion expressed as customs and not ideologies, a vigorous internal competition balanced by a horizontal hierarchy where most find a place unless they are bad, and a notion of the transcendental as a means to appreciating natural order and also opening the doorway to the faint light of the metaphysical, so that those who possess a genius aptitude and moral attraction to such things can follow. It is not unknown to us moderns that these are the best societies; we simply refuse to indulge in them because of our pretence of individualism and the political philosophy of egalitarianism that we use to enforce this pretence on others.

Our path toward this saner world involves first an inward conditioning to see that what our intuition knows is true is more important than our fears for ourselves, and through this, to realize that a more orderly civilization and more balanced/ harmonious world will benefit us to a greater degree than any direct reward to ourselves ever can. This will start with a few lone thinkers, spread to the top 2-5% of the population by natural leadership ability, and eventually become a cultural norm. As we watch liberal democracy collapse in a spreading mire of corruption, ineptitude, social decay, misery, atomization, and libertinism, this future in the past becomes inevitable.

9. **D.A.R.G.:** Is it possible to name a few individuals that would come archetypally close to a practical and successful application of Esoteric Nihilism, heroes or exemplars, so to speak? What and how does each of them achieve this place? More importantly, what can we learn from them, not only in terms of what they did, but of what they left out?

Brett Stevens: Let me speak only of a few, since most live and die anonymously, having been content to influence those around them locally. Marcus Aurelius, Johannes Eckhart, and William S. Burroughs come to mind, with the latter two being intensely focused on the monist metaphysics of the universe and the former an archetypal genial agnostic. Their thinking was to avoid the innate mental control exerted by the herd, to separate what was actually true from what we wished would be true so that our fears would go away, and then to apply that through knowledge of both the law of attraction and the underlying generative structure inherent to our universe. Our best strategy is to emulate that example, but in the interest of esotericism, that statement alone should suffice. Those who want to know will find a way to know and by knowing, they will meet the universe halfway and it will do the same, making incarnate what they desire that is also in parallel to the logic of the world. Interestingly, none of them would have identified as anything like an "esoteric nihilist," which shows us why the nihilist theory on language is superior; you and I, and maybe some of our readers, understand what these tokens mean, but others use other tokens to mean the same thing, and what speaks to us across history is how those understandings are expressed through works and deeds more than statements of prescriptive logic.

Did you love *Gradus ad Phlegethon*? Then you should read *Kosmokrator* by Yperion Press!

KOSMOKRATOR

Issue 1

YPERION

Flagship journal of Yperion Press, focusing on remote viewing and the out-of-body experience as a means of expanding power in the world.